"Little did I know that it was possible to cr[...] exact time. As a man doing a swan dive [...] needed this book is. Being formed into Christ's love and mercy can often be most difficult in these years, and McNiel and Hague have given us a trusted path forward. Get out the Kleenex for this one, folks. And let the inner healing begin."

A.J. Swoboda, associate professor of Bible and theology at Bushnell University and author of *The Gift of Thorns*

"What do we do when faith collapses? Acquiesce and walk away? Or deny and double down? Are those our only options? While it can seem so at times, gratefully they are not. There is a better way, one that discerns the work of the triune God amid the collapse and leads to God's greatest good for our lives: Christlikeness. We need wise guides to help us discover that path and follow it. Catherine McNiel and Jason Hague are just such guides, and I couldn't be more grateful for this work. It'll be on my short list of recommended resources for deconstructing parishioners."

Andrew Arndt, lead pastor of New Life East in Colorado Springs and author of *All Flame*

"If you grew up in church with a vibrant faith but have found yourself wounded, disillusioned, or in a mid-faith crisis as an adult, this book is for you. Catherine McNiel and Jason Hague are experienced, wise, and compassionate guides who will give you confidence and hope. *Mid-Faith Crisis* is full of helpful personal stories, spiritual exercises, and reflections to help you find your spiritual footing again."

Matt Mikalatos, author of *God with Us* and *Imaginary Jesus*

"*Mid-Faith Crisis* is that rare blend of prophetic, pastoral, funny and poignant, truly a 'for such a time as this' kind of book. McNiel and Hague, with unromanticized vulnerability and theological precision, invite the doubter, the deconstructionist, the disillusioned, and the deeply seasoned Christian into a faith that can exist both after and within crisis. For anyone who has been hurt by but still longs to find a way to love this wild thing called the church, and for anyone who wants to follow Jesus without the tired and clichéd trappings, you'll find yourself seen, known, and led in these pages."

Aubrey Sampson, teaching pastor, podcast host, and author of *What We Find in the Dark*

"This business of managing a crisis of faith is filled with sadness, anger, and disillusionment, but mostly it's an experience of deep loneliness. McNeil and Hague have written in such a way that they are encouraging companions for such a journey. By the time they are done, they have helped us all remember that we were never as alone as it might have seemed."

Marty Solomon, creator of *The BEMA Podcast* and author of *Asking Better Questions of the Bible*

"Catherine McNiel and Jason Hague are refreshingly honest about their own faith journeys and are not afraid of asking difficult questions about church trauma, fallen spiritual leaders, the death of loved ones, and challenging health diagnoses. This book doesn't sugarcoat these experiences but rather shares a real hope and pathway through to a more settled faith on the other side. This gem of a book is for everyone who is walking through a mid-faith crisis, is going to, or knows someone who is! So grab at least two copies of this book—one for yourself and one for a friend. You'll be so glad you did!"

Joyce Koo Dalrymple, founder of Refuge for Strength and author of *Women of the New Testament*

FINDING A PATH THROUGH DOUBT,
DISILLUSIONMENT, AND DEAD ENDS

MID-FAITH CRISIS

CATHERINE McNIEL AND JASON HAGUE

ivp

An imprint of InterVarsity Press
Downers Grove, Illinois

InterVarsity Press
P.O. Box 1400 | Downers Grove, IL 60515-1426
ivpress.com | email@ivpress.com

InterVarsity Press® is the publishing division of InterVarsity Christian Fellowship/USA®. For more information, visit intervarsity.org.

All Scripture quotations, unless otherwise indicated, are taken from The Holy Bible, New International Version®, NIV®. Copyright © 1973, 1978, 1984, 2011 by Biblica, Inc.™ Used by permission of Zondervan. All rights reserved worldwide. www.zondervan.com. The "NIV" and "New International Version" are trademarks registered in the United States Patent and Trademark Office by Biblica, Inc.™

Published in association with the literary agent Don Gates of The Gates Group, www.the-gates-group.com.

"Engine Against Th'Almightie" from *After Prayer* by Malcolm Guite is © Malcolm Guite, 2019. Published by Canterbury Press. Used by permission. rights@hymnsam.co.uk.

While any stories in this book are true, some names and identifying information may have been changed to protect the privacy of individuals.

The publisher cannot verify the accuracy or functionality of website URLs used in this book beyond the date of publication.

Cover design: Faceout Studio, Spencer Fuller
Interior design: Jeanna Wiggins
Image: © Visoot Uthairam / Moment via Getty Images

ISBN 978-1-5140-1036-5 (print) | ISBN 978-1-5140-1037-2 (digital)

Printed in the United States of America ♾

Library of Congress Cataloging-in-Publication Data
A catalog record for this book is available from the Library of Congress.

31 30 29 28 27 26 25 | 12 11 10 9 8 7 6 5 4 3 2 1

To every person

in the trenches of mid-faith crisis,

we wrote this book for you.

Never shall I forget those moments
that murdered my God and my soul
and turned my dreams to ashes.

ELIE WIESEL

CONTENTS

PART 1

SETTING THE STAGE(S)

1

LET'S START WITH A MEME

A meme pops up on social media every now and then: How It Started v. How It's Going. Couples post first-date snapshots alongside celebratory wedding pictures. Parents post their newborn baby alongside their college graduate. One astronaut framed an old picture of his childhood self in a cardboard-box rocket ship next to a picture of his grown-man self flying a real NASA space shuttle.

We depict less celebratory things with this meme too: breakups, loss, decline. Things that started strong and fancy ending weak and laughable. But whichever direction the photos take us, we enjoy the contrast of time passing, change happening. We smile proudly, laugh uncomfortably. It's all so true, so relatable.

What would our faith look like in a How It Started vs. How It's Going meme? What was our fresh, hopeful picture at the beginning—and how do we look now?

For many of us . . . well, it's not pretty. Whether we began the faith journey in childhood or adulthood, we started full of earnest faith, hope, and love. But life has proven to be complicated, and for many of us the faith we had at the beginning couldn't hold up to the challenge. Over time, our religious energy and excitement fizzled. Our prayer muscles atrophied. Our trust was shaken. The songs, books, verses, and even beliefs we once loved now vividly remind us of painful losses and disappointments.

What happened? Why the stark juxtaposition between how we started out in the faith and how it's going now? Simply put, we hit a crisis or two, or three. A mid-faith crisis, you might call it. As you've likely noticed, this is a common tale.

But before we jump into all that, let us introduce ourselves—and show you a bit of how it started and how it's going for the two of us.

JASON: HOW IT STARTED

For me, it started with bright lights and TV cameras.

The year was 1987. I was eight years old, traveling up the East Coast with a performing arts troupe made up of thirty neon-clad kids and chaperones. We didn't just believe in God; we were on fire for God. We performed in churches—Sunday services, youth groups, Vacation Bible Schools—and they loved us. But there was one extra-special stop on our itinerary.

"We're going to be on *The 700 Club!*" we exclaimed to our grandparents over long-distance phone lines. They gushed and gloated. Their grandchildren performing on the most popular Christian news program in the world? They just *knew* God was going to do big things. In between songs, I was going to be interviewed on air. Me! Speaking into the same mic Pat Robertson, Billy Graham, and Kathy Lee Gifford had used at one time or another. Live, under the lights, cameras rolling. I had made the big time.

Ben Kinchlow introduced us. "Here they are: The King's Kids."

The lights came on, the music began, and we were off, singing and dancing and cheerfully proclaiming our lifelong intention to follow Christ.

Lord, we will live our lives for You,
Serve You faithfully like you want us to![1]

It was such an easy promise to make. The words just rolled off our tongues.

The audience ate us up, and why wouldn't they? We were sincere in our faith, zealous in our proclamation, and glimmering with youth. Wherever we performed, the saints of our parents' and grandparents' generations gave us the same praise: God's got big plans for you kids!

Then it was time for my interview. I don't remember Kinchlow's exact question, but it was something like: How did you get picked to be here?

My answer I remember vividly, because my mother pulled out the VHS tape at every dinner party. "That's hard to say," I told him, "because they're not really the ones who picked me. Because God called on me, and he's the one who picked me."

Kinchlow blinked and took a step back. The audience gave something of a gasp. I knew I had impressed them.

That answer, along with Kinchlow's flummoxed response, became legendary (at least, in my circles). "I saw your interview. You stole the show!" grownups would tell me for months after. "You give me so much hope for our future."

The videotape was destroyed in a flood (thanks be to God), but the prognostication rang in my ears for decades: "God's got big plans for you, young man! You're going to change the world!"

JASON: HOW IT'S GOING

Thirty-seven years after I polished my halo under those TV lights, after the world glimpsed my staggering potential, I have not changed the world.

In many ways, faith proved somewhat of a letdown early on. Life in my twenties and thirties was not about greatness and all about waiting. My wife and I went into full-time ministry just a few years into our marriage, and I went on to become a pastor. I was waiting for God to make good on all the promises I'd invested in. But while I waited, troubles came, and I was not prepared.

The first trouble was with my two sons. Sam was born with a heart condition that would require open-heart surgery while he was still an infant. While we were trying to keep Sam alive, Jack, his three-year-old brother, was diagnosed with autism. The kind with hard behaviors and meltdowns. The kind without words.

That initial combination pushed me into something else I wasn't prepared for: depression. I felt spiritually and emotionally drained. Even after Sam's heart condition was mostly resolved, the sorrow lingered as I considered my grim future with Jack, who was incapable of conversing with me. I had always been a people person, but soon I found myself isolating. I kept wondering why God was letting me languish in this kind of pain.

As the years went by and our family crises multiplied and intensified, another trouble set in: disillusionment. The evangelical church in America was being torn apart by political allegiances and scandal. Many of the communities, beliefs, and practices of faith that I'd always leaned on during times of hardship were crumbling. Heroes and mentors I had revered for almost two decades were being unmasked as abusers, a far, far cry from the Christlike path I thought we were walking together.

For the next few years my spiritual confidence ebbed and flowed. I was not prepared for any of this. What happened to the "big plans" God had for me? Somedays, it felt like I had fallen victim to a cosmic con, as if my faith was nothing more than a bait-and-switch.

I weathered the storm for a while, but then came the deaths. Two women, both dear friends of mine, were diagnosed with cancer while they were still young, in their thirties and forties. They were like sisters to me, and I lost them both.

That was when the full brunt of faith crisis hit me. Far from changing the world for Christ, I was awash in a multitude of griefs, accusations, and fears. I didn't dare tell anyone what was going on inside me. Instead, I went on with my work as a pastor, dutifully writing my sermons, hoping and praying that my secret grappling wouldn't disqualify me from ministry, wouldn't lead me away from the God I still loved and mostly trusted.

I had already lost my confidence. Then I lost my sisters. Now I feared I might lose Jesus too.

CATHERINE: HOW IT STARTED

My faith began more simply than Jason's—and with fewer lights and cameras. I grew up in a dairy-farming community in rural Wisconsin, a small life in the small town my family moved to when my dad became the pastor of a small church in town. I was just four years old when our moving truck pulled up to the old parsonage, so this tight-knit community was the only home I knew.

I loved that my dad was the pastor. I loved listening to him bounce sermon ideas off us at dinner, loved beaming at him from the second row as my brother and I appeared in yet another sermon illustration. He was a great pastor, a servant in every sense of the word. He had a way of connecting the ancient wisdom of a text to the tangible needs of the people he deeply knew and genuinely loved.

Growing up as transplants in this multigenerational community—and far from our own extended family—the older folks become my grandparents, the younger families my aunts, uncles, and cousins. The church couldn't afford to pay much, but there were other perks. Home was just around the corner from church, which was also my dad's office, my school, and my second home. We visited the parishioners' farms in the evenings, dipping our buckets into their milk vats and bringing milk home to drink. Chatting with the farmers in their milking parlors, we "helped" milk the Holsteins. Our freezer filled with meat during hunting season and our pantry with canned vegetables during growing season. We were invited to spend Sunday dinners and holiday meals around their tables, with their families. We were known and loved; we cared for others and were cared for in return. To me, everything about this community was safe, was home.

At my tiny Christian school, my desk was a small, wooden cubicle, side-by-side with many others lining the walls of the schoolroom. Our self-guided lessons were easy and uplifting, and the wooden dividers that hemmed us in didn't feel restrictive. The carefully constructed walls and the carefully constructed curriculum embodied the warm, safe cocoon of Christian community, my Christian community.

CATHERINE: HOW IT'S GOING

When I turned twelve, it all turned upside down, all at once. My dad walked into an elders' meeting one night; when he left, we had two weeks to pack up and leave town. There would be no grace, no help, and precious few friends who would stick with us as we left. We just had to go. Leave the house, leave the church, leave my school, leave the community, leave my adopted grandmothers and grandfathers, leave my friends. Just get out.

I suppose the goal, from the church's standpoint, was to make this all as noiseless as possible, to erase us as entirely as they could. We were to leave no trace, nothing for anyone to think about or feel once we were gone.

This isn't the place to dissect the reasons behind the elders' decision; suffice to say there were real problems to address and change needed to happen. But erasure is rarely the best way to enact change or solve problems long term. It is utterly disorienting for a child, having one place that holds all your relationships, all your memories, all your identity . . . and then suddenly and irrevocably being banned from that place—and that people. There were devastating losses like shelter, salary, and healthcare. But there were so many more intangible deaths, of everything familiar, everything that told me how to understand who I was and where I belonged. Once those two weeks passed, we were not invited to come back, and very few people stayed in touch. The door slammed shut behind us and locked on our way out.

There are laws now to make this level of destabilization and erasure more difficult to implement. We're taught to view pastors differently now too, as humans with human families and human needs. But back then, in our story, we were just sent away. We lost everything in the process.

That callous decision, made by the fathers and grandfathers of my church community but carried out collectively by everyone I knew, thrust me into an early mid-faith crisis. I knew for sure, at age twelve, that folks were never what they seemed, never truly trustworthy, that my family and I deserved to be abandoned, at any time, for any reason, and therefore might be again. How could I feel safe in any relationship, much less inside a community of faith? How could I ever join a group of Christians in worship and fully, genuinely lend my voice to theirs?

MID-FAITH CRISIS

If you're reading this book, chances are you can relate to some aspect of these stories. You've had your own mid-faith crisis or two; you might be in the middle of one right now. Maybe the crisis came up suddenly and blind-sided you, as Catherine's did. Maybe you've been thrust out of your community, exiled and rejected by the most toxic people Christendom has to offer. Maybe you've been locked outside in the cold, and all you can hear from inside the church is the verse, chorus, and bridge of yet another hollow anthem you'd do anything to avoid.

Or maybe your story is more like Jason's. Maybe your crisis arrived not with a single heartbreak but with an accumulation of wounds and doubts, compounded by soul-level exhaustion. We absorb those blows for a while. Months, years, decades, even. We keep going to church on Sundays, keep serving, keep loving, keep praying. We may even keep preaching! But eventually, one too many straws lands on the back of that tired camel—one more dreaded diagnosis, one more fallen hero—and the whole edifice falls apart.

Maybe your story is quite different from either of ours. We have friends who realized they had been taught to view God as more hateful than loving, and to despise (not love) their neighbors as themselves—and no longer wanted to live or believe this way. Other friends realized they were in churches that worshiped and emulated power, patriarchy, or patriotism over Jesus. Too many people we know have been physically or emotionally harmed by pastors or Christian leaders. Plenty of friends were taught doctrines that just didn't hold up to scrutiny. And some simply describe their faith as melting away unexpectedly, like sugar in the rain.

So back to that How It Started vs. How It's Going meme. What does it look like for our faith journey so far? Some of these words might describe how it started for you:

- Hopeful
- Joyful
- Excited
- Committed to a faith community
- Compelled by a sense of meaning and fulfillment
- Changed by God's love
- Inspired by heroes of the faith
- Spiritual euphoria
- Certainty
- Belief
- Tangible fruits of the Spirit

And how it's going?

- Disappointed
- Fallen heroes
- Poor treatment by the church
- Disillusionment
- Broken promises
- Scandal
- Hypocrisy
- Years of suffering
- Prayers unanswered
- Doubt
- God feeling distant
- Truth revealed as lies

Do any of these descriptors feel familiar? If so, you're not alone. We've been there too. We are there too, right in the trenches with you. And we're convinced of two things: We can't stay here and aren't willing to go backward. We can't pretend we haven't seen and know what we have seen and know.

What options are left? We could leave the faith. That's what many folks we know have done, plus a host of high-profile Christians. When it gets too much—this soul-crushing weight of deconstruction and detangling, of wrestling with God, the Scriptures, and the church—we can walk away and be done with it all. For many, de-conversion feels like the only path forward.

But is there another honest path we could take, one allowing us to tell the truth yet search for faith? We were curious. We aren't the first people to hit a mid-faith crisis after all. We're not the first generation to deconstruct in adulthood what we'd been taught in our childhood or teen years, not by a long shot. Generations of believers have wrestled through questions like the ones we're asking now and have proposed truly compelling answers to those questions.

So we took a step back and did some digging. What we learned validated our own experiences of doubt and pain while also giving us hope for the future. We'd love to show you what we found, tell you a lot more stories, and consider together where we go from here.

Will you come along?

PRACTICE

|||||||||||||||||||||||||||||||||||||||||||||||||||| *How It Started v. How It's Going*

Throughout this book, we'll explore a few practical components of faith for moving forward. We know all too well that some of the faith practices we were initially taught and held on to for years are not what we need now or in the future, yet we don't want to be formed by atrophy. If what we offer in these sections feels life giving, use or adapt them in whatever way feels useful to you.

Find a quiet place and consider the How It Started vs. How It's Going pictures from your faith journey. Depending on how you explore and express yourself, you might use words, art, or music to depict these—or whatever you prefer.

- How would you describe the way your faith started?
- How would you describe the way your faith is going now?
- What would you like your faith to grow into, eventually? What words or images would you use to describe that place?

||||||||||||||||||||||||||||||||||||||||||||||||||||||||||||||||||||||||||||||||||||||||||||||||||||||||||||||||||||||||||

2

STAGES OF FAITH

If you walk into a church building during Sunday school hour, you'll likely find a few things going on at once. In one room, preschoolers sit in a circle, hearing a story of Jesus' love while munching crackers and sipping from juice boxes. In another room, loud music plays in the background as teens are challenged to consider their identity in Christ, or plan an energetic service project surrounded by stacks of pizza boxes. In yet another room, adults dig into a Bible study specifically chosen by the group because the challenging topic has left questions lingering in their minds for decades.

In each room, God is being sought after and worshiped— but in a way that meets the developmental needs and strengths of different life stages. We know from experience that we're wired to approach faith differently at different times.

Most of us have also sat in a room where at least one person confessed: "None of this makes sense to me anymore. I think my faith is falling apart."

Most churches don't have a Sunday school classroom for the life stage called "Reconsidering Everything I Was Taught

About God"—but maybe we should. For some reason, we expect that our faith will grow in a steady trajectory, or at least that things will continue on the way they started. (God is faithful to complete the good work he began in us, after all!)

But that's not what normal growth patterns look like. Health—in our bodies, gardens, minds, and even relationships—requires occasional growth spurts and times of dormancy, times that might even look like decline.

Researchers and scholars of religion and human development have noticed that normal patterns of faith involve highs along with lows, disintegration as well as growth. Just as there are natural, predictable cycles in human physical and emotional development, there are natural, predictable cycles in human faith development. Importantly, these are not classified as increasingly "Bigger!" and "Better!" Seasons of dormancy and decline are normal and even a sign of health. A healthy faith simply does not move upward in a straight line.

James Fowler, a scholar of religion and psychology, identified six unique developmental stages that people may encounter if they continue in faith for a lifetime. His fourth stage, rarely reached before middle adulthood, is marked by questioning and doubting everything. Janet Hagberg and Robert Guelich's *The Critical Journey* described five stages, while M. Scott Peck and Brian McLaren each boiled their stages down to four.[1] Regardless, each researcher found a similar theme: somewhere deep into the maturing process we hit a wall. There is a season after we have things figured out when everything crumbles apart.

In *Praying the Psalms,* Walter Brueggemann described these inevitable crises of faith by using the terms *disorientation* and *reorientation.*[2] He offered a plethora of examples from the book of Psalms in which the writer, lost in confusion, rages against his enemies and against God, only to come out on the other side with a very different view from where he started. Bruce Demarest expands on this to include seasons of orientation when we (believe we) see clearly, seasons of distress when we are disoriented, all leading ultimately to seasons of redemption: stronger and more mature views that make better sense of God and reality than we had before. Brueggemann describes these shifting seasons as "movements" and notes that they happen not just once but many times in our lives.

The book you are holding in your hands is not a work of religious psychology; however, the idea that faith has predictable stages that include disorientation and disintegration is essential to our stories. So, let's examine a common life cycle of faith. Rather than leaning on any individual scholar or theory, we're going to synthesize them into our own four stages: Inherited Faith, Confident Faith, Mid-Faith, and Conscious Faith.

STAGE ONE: INHERITED FAITH

Let's imagine you have a young friend named Hannah, who is in this first stage, Inherited Faith. A few years ago, Hannah wondered if she might see Jonah's whale at the beach, and if God could see her even when she played hide-and-seek. Since then, she's moved beyond the literalism of early childhood but still accepts the basic faith and worldview pillars she was taught without question.[3]

This Inherited Faith stage is where we all start: young children embracing everything we are taught by our parents and community. We form pictures of the divine that are part cartoon, part magic: God is old. God is big. God has a beard. As we grow, we begin wrapping our minds around the stories of our community's faith and give those stories simple, very literal interpretations, which form our unquestioned foundation of reality—and of ourselves. We see this at work in Catherine's Christian school cubicles where she learned simplified lessons about faith and morality, as well as in Jason's free-spirited, big-promising songs. This season of faith is uncomplicated. Reality is very knowable, and there is no tension or disagreement. We memorize the doctrines to prove what we have been taught and are trained to recite them when required. We need this foundational stage at the proper developmental time, to gain a feeling of security and rootedness for the long haul. Normal, healthy, human development requires spending time in this concrete, black-and-white mindset.

But, of course, we cannot stay with our Inherited Faith forever.

STAGE TWO: CONFIDENT FAITH

Hannah has an older cousin named Adam. In high school and college, Adam interacted with ideas and examples of faith that compelled him to lean in and intentionally give his life to God. He studies the teachings of Jesus and of his faith tradition, alongside others and on his own, and is increasingly viewed as a leader in his church. He is known as a man who takes his faith seriously and is building his life, career, and family with God at the center.

Most of us make this leap into stage two in adolescence or early adulthood, and we stay there for many years, maybe even the rest of our lives. In Confident Faith, we take what we have been given and look for an identity, a place to belong in the concreteness of our religious understanding and community, a way to make it our own—just as in other areas of life we begin making sense of ourselves through the eyes of our peers and in the groups that accept us. Through rites of passage (confirmation, baptism, or bar mitzvah, for example) or community experiences (Bible camp, youth group, youth conferences, internet circles) we find ourselves called forth and named, and our beliefs crystallize into convictions that change our lives. We put our feet down onto solid religious and ideological constructs that make sense of the world and our place in it while providing a path we can follow through the harrowing transitional years between childhood and adulthood. This may be a time to double down on what we received from our earliest influences, or a way to differentiate from them through modification or even conversion to different ways of thinking and living. Many of us carry powerful memories from this stage that buoy us through the storms and trials to come.

For Jason, this looked like going to Christian high school and being baptized. It looked like marrying his wife in his father's church, going to Bible school and adopting the theological convictions of his teachers, then growing even more convinced of them. Jason entered the stage of Confident Faith during adolescence and settled into that neighborhood for many years. He found an identity as a son of God, a member of the church, and a thinker of sound, godly thoughts. It was a positive season of life for him—as it is meant to be—with vivid, compelling faith and family as the centerpiece.

This is an important thing to emphasize: these developmental stages are intended to be empowering and life giving, and certainly they are necessary and unavoidable. They provide years if not decades of steady-going life and faith—as they are meant to do. If you grow into Confident Faith, you know who you are, what you believe, where you belong, and how you can make a meaningful contribution to the world. This is the stuff of growing up, of launching and leading a fulfilling adult life.

Furthermore, most churches and Christian institutions are built with this very stage in mind, investing in children and teenagers in order to usher them into their adult place in the faith. As a result, many of us assume that faith has only these two stages: the one we inherited as children and the one we make our own in adulthood. If we reach adulthood with our faith intact, we assume we are "grown up" in the faith and our life cycle is complete. The only task now is to stay the course.

That's what Adam is hoping to do as he takes his young family to church every Sunday. He wants to hold on, fight the good fight, keep the faith. But this may prove to be more difficult than he expects.

STAGE THREE: MID-FAITH

Adam has a friend he worries about named Jeremy. Jeremy is asking questions that sound dangerous, and there is often pain or anger in his voice. He points to fallen leaders and toxic teachings; he wonders if there really is an eternal hell where God tortures his creatures, and if God only loves Christians. Actually, he wonders if God is even truly loving—or if an all-powerful being really exists. Jeremy appreciates his friends' attempts to encourage him but ultimately isn't helped by the answers they find so comforting.

Jeremy is neck deep in Stage Three: Mid-Faith, and it's no surprise he's struggling. This stage is nearly always kindled by life's heartaches and upheaval. Some people face new evidence about their faith communities, history, or doctrines that throws them for a loop. Or they encounter compelling points of view that challenge their earlier convictions, and they realize the answers they stood on weren't as solid as they believed. Others get worn down by the burdens and troubles of life and wonder how the good news adds any goodness to the real world.

However we arrive at Mid-Faith, this stage does not feel like growth: it shatters many of our earlier faith illusions and brings pain. There's no way to reset the clock, no way to unsee all we've seen or put Pandora back in her box. This is why we're calling it a mid-faith crisis. And while Fowler, Brueggemann, Hagberg, and many others use different names, they find the same foundational reality to be true: the path of faith inherently includes seasons that feel like the death of faith. We cannot deny or avoid this. The only way out is through.

As we saw in the previous chapter, the two of us hit this stage at very different times and in vastly different ways. Catherine's mid-faith crisis hit in childhood, and it hit hard, forming her origin story. When she was exiled at age twelve, she was left with a deep sense of rejection, unworthiness, and disorientation. She lost the opportunity to be rooted and grounded in the soils of a confident faith, to be named by a community of faith. Her disillusionment, you might say, set in before she was fully illusioned.

Jason took a more typical route. He entered into crisis more slowly, death by a thousand paper cuts. Each pain—the loss of certainty, the unanswered prayers, the failure of trusted mentors—shook another brick loose in the foundation of his faith until one last blow sent him reeling.

If you're in stage three, Mid-Faith, you might feel as though something precious and necessary is being yanked away, melting rapidly, or being flushed down the drain. None of it feels like a choice, and certainly not like growth or health. Our spirits cry out: What's wrong? Who is at fault? Did I fail? Did God fail? What happened to my faith?

The experience of mid-faith crisis is a wilderness. We feel alone with our questions, alienated from the answers and people that gave us life.

But we have good news, friend: we are not alone. This thing that hit so hard and so unexpectedly is, in truth, so common that each researcher we studied identified it as a predictable marker on a mature person's spiritual journey. This season is neither private failure nor personal discovery. It has a name, and millions of people across every century have felt it, gone through it, and survived it.

In other words, you're not walking by yourself, and you're not a hopeless case. On the contrary, you're probably right on schedule. There is more ahead in this journey of faith development if we are willing to keep going. For all its pain and disruption, the mid-faith crisis of stage three does not have to signal the death of belief or spirituality. There is a pathway through, and a stronger, more settled life of faith on the other side.

STAGE FOUR: CONSCIOUS FAITH

While Jeremy grapples with his mid-faith questions, he runs into a former neighbor, Martha. To his surprise, Martha isn't put off by the questions Jeremy raises, nor does she dismiss them. She seems grounded in both reality and hope in a way Jeremy hasn't encountered, able to hold both the beauty and pain of life in one hand with gratitude and calm, acknowledging all that we cannot know or control.

Martha and Jeremy begin to meet for coffee each week. Jeremy doesn't always agree with Martha's ideas, yet he can't help but respect them. Martha doesn't hide behind her groundedness to avoid his questions, nor does she gloss over the injustices and deep suffering she has experienced. Instead, she wades all the way in, meeting him and others where they are, making small but persistent differences in the lives and systems around her.

Martha only reached stage four after surviving her own barrage of crises. She suffered years of personal and religious trauma and experienced the loss of friends and family. She asked many of the same questions Jeremy is asking now. And, while she's wrestled down a few answers over the years, she's primarily made peace with uncertainty and found healing in beauty and mystery.

Stage four—what we're calling Conscious Faith—is marked with a sense of coming back home and feeling at peace in your own skin. Should we arrive here, we'll begin to feel comfortable with the limits of logic and the realities of paradox. We'll feel present with ourselves in a way we rarely have before and bring that same comfort to our relationships with others, to the harsh realities of life—and to our relationship with God.

We won't say much about stage four right now except to encourage you that a genuine and life-giving faith does lie on the other side of the dark valley of a mid-faith crisis. While not everyone will want to search it out, it is possible to get there. Conscious Faith is largely populated by folks like Martha: men and women who put in their time doing honest wrestling with life and with God and will forever bear the marks of suffering. But they are survivors, and victors too. They have been humbled, but they have been raised up. And in the process they have found peace and a deep, lasting rootedness.

WHERE WE GO FROM HERE

When we find ourselves hitting the wall of mid-faith crisis, it's easy to look behind and see all that we lost. The How It Started and How It's Going pictures are stark and all too clear. But imagining what might lie ahead? That feels impossible. From here we can't glimpse anything except the remnants of a faith we can no longer authentically own.

Rarely are churches or ministries designed or even able to help us sort through these new doubts and questions. There's no "What to Expect" series, or video curriculum on "Preparing for (Faith) Adolescence." That's why we panic when it happens, and why our faith leaders panic alongside us (and may ask us to backpedal, if we can). We were trained to grow from Inherited Faith to Confident Faith, then expected to stay the course. There was no game plan for anything after that.

Our goal in this book isn't to foist you into a faith crisis if you aren't in one or to push you out into a bright new reality if you are. We simply want to open a discussion that might help fill that gap—to be honest about the low places of faith and normalize the idea that this stage of upheaval is common and even necessary.

When it comes to physical human development, we would never believe stagnation was a sign of health, would we? If our five-year-old did not mature beyond the baby stage, or if our teenagers skipped over the hormonal changes that turn them into adults, we would seek drastic medical interventions. We instinctively know progression is rife with losses and challenges. Yet we embrace all the upheaval for we can picture our destination and know that it is good.

Remember your baby teeth falling out? This childhood rite of passage is a good and necessary transition. But it's awful! Mouths start bleeding in the middle of recess, smiles look funny in family photos, and taking a bite from a juicy apple is impossible. But the fact is, grownups need bigger, stronger teeth than babies can handle. Out with the milk teeth, in with the steak teeth. We lose something that has been good and necessary to make room for something longer lasting to take its place.

Friend, this is true also in the life of faith. What we had was good and necessary, and the sudden loss can feel like we're dying, falling apart. But this does not mean the end, does not mean failure, does not mean we are cut off from God. Rather, we may find something stronger, something longer lasting moving in to take its place: a faith that will make peace with so much of the complexity and mystery we have wrestled with throughout the years.

Making that space is what we aim to do in this book. We'll share stories of mid-faith crisis and the sparks that lit the flames, facets of our faith that stopped working and pushed us into crisis. We won't hide from them or sugarcoat them but haul them all the way out into the light. We'll see that how it started is most definitely not how it's going. But then we'll ask other honest questions: What comes next? Where do we go from here? We won't flinch from those questions either.

In the next chapter, we'll talk about the crushing power of doubt. In stage one, Inherited Faith, there was no reason to question the veracity of what our trusted guides taught us. As we grew into stage two, Confident Faith, many of us encountered doubt but were taught to tamp it down at all costs. Now, in stage three, Mid-Faith, doubt barges in uninvited and puts his feet up on the coffee table. We can't use the old tactics anymore; we can't ignore him and hope he leaves. He's not leaving. But we don't need to be afraid of doubt either. We will find a way forward with doubt.

This is what we'll be doing throughout the book, looking at a variety of sparks that kindle the mid-faith crisis—because we've caught a glimpse of hope that there's life, and faith, on the other side.

PRACTICE

IIIIIIIIIIIIIIIIIIIIIIIIIIIIIIIIIIIIIIIIIIIIIIIIIIIIIIIIIIIII *Finding Yourself on the Journey*

If you were taught to view faith as a one-time decision made, or a journey that always and only went in an upward direction, you may not have been equipped for the lifelong task of spiritual formation, of growing and changing not only in maturity but also in perspective, needs, and practices. If the idea of faith as a journey—with expected valleys, upheavals, and even crises—is new to you, take a moment to consider where you are now and where you would like to go.

We propose that even significant faith crises may be an expected and even healthy step in the journey of faith. Have you considered this before? What thoughts or feelings do you experience as you consider that idea?

Take a moment to reflect on the stages of faith.

Where would you consider yourself now? What are some of the life experiences that brought you here?

What did each of these stages look like for you? What were some helpful and unhelpful aspects that you remember from each?

Table 2.1. The stages of faith and how they manifest

Distinctions	Inherited Faith Hannah	Confident Faith Adam	Mid-Faith Jeremy	Conscious Faith Martha
Feels like . . .	reality	maturity, ownership	shaky, out of control, like losing faith	calm and grounded
Time frame	from birth onward	adolescence and onward	rarely begins before mid-adulthood	rarely begins before mid-life
Entrance	birth	formal or informal rite of passage	crisis or questions	like a light at the end of a tunnel
View of God	magical, authority	personal, inspiring	uncertain, suspicious	mystery, goodness
View of self and faith	un-self-conscious	belonging, decision making	confused, doubting, backsliding	comfortable, healing, peaceful
Motivation	right or wrong	in group or out group	authentic or false	connected or separate
Center	story	identity	questions	complexity
Key words	story, simple, belief, black-and-white, literal, early childhood, trusting	concrete, grownup, belonging, ownership, identity, personal, community, doctrine, experience, conviction	individuated, theoretical, skeptical, doubt, questions, disorientation, deconstruction, honesty, authenticity, shaken	comfortable, awakened, at home, at peace, transcending logic, paradox, comfort with self and others, peering into mystery, healing, connectedness

Have you met someone who exemplified the qualities in the stages you have not yet reached? What is attractive to you about that person's faith or that stage in general? What is confusing or threatening?

||||||||||||||||||||||||||||||||||||||||||||||||||||||||||||||||||||||||||| *Something to Listen To*

- "Deconstruction," Lecrae
- "All the Way My Savior Leads Me," Rich Mullins

Something to Read

- *Where the Light Fell: A Memoir,* Philip Yancey
- *All My Knotted-Up Life: A Memoir,* Beth Moore
- *Unfollow: A Memoir of Loving and Leaving the Westboro Baptist Church,* Megan Phelps-Roper
- *Seasons of the Soul: Stages of Spiritual Development,* Bruce Demarest

PART 2

THE
CRISIS

3

WHEN DOUBT CREPT IN

If you had asked me (Jason) to define faith as an eight-year-old, back when I was a television star and spiritual guru, I probably would have answered that faith was believing really, really, really hard that something was true. It would have been more precious than that, and you would have swooned as I polished my halo a little brighter. But my answer would have been wrong. And no wonder: it came from fairy tales.

There's a moment in *Peter Pan* when Tinkerbell is on the brink of death, and Peter—the boy who never grew up—revives her. He performs this miracle not with a kiss, nor with CPR, but with the force of his intellectual commitment. According to the narrator, this "belief" is essential: if anyone says they *don't* believe in fairies, one fairy, somewhere, will die.

"I do believe in fairies. I do! I do!" Peter cries, mustering up as much sincerity as he can. "I do believe in fairies. I do! I do!" And with that heartfelt confession, his pixie sidekick is restored to life.[1]

That's more or less what faith looked like to me as a boy. I believed in Jesus, and I believed really, really hard. I knew God was real and the Bible was true, and nothing could talk me out of it. I spent my entire childhood in a God-soaked environment. My parents were in full-time vocational ministry, and I went to a Christian school from kindergarten on. The truth of the gospel flowed through my veins, and I knew it was true. Nobody could talk me out of it. No one could.

By the time I got to high school, I was so certain. Two girls in my class grew quite sick of my heavy-handed confidence and self-assurance. They weren't sure what they believed about the big questions in life, and I hassled them, argued with them. But despite all my sarcasm and holiest diatribes, they remained strangely hesitant.

I carried this sense of Christian rightness with me into adulthood. Thankfully, after taking a few lumps in life, I matured and mostly stopped being so annoying. But going into ministry in my early twenties, I remained as confident as ever that God was real, the Bible was true, and Jesus was the Savior of the world. I had the answers! I had examined the math up close and nothing else made sense. "I do believe in Jesus. I do! I do!" I was convinced. I was sure.

Until I wasn't.

HOW IT'S GOING

It was the most predictable development, really: life got to me. Heartbreak and disillusionment hit; something dislodged inside my soul. It wasn't my faith—it was my sureness. The fact that I thought they were the same thing was the problem.

For the first time in my entire life, I wasn't sure I was right about my religious convictions. I wasn't sure if God was good or was hearing my prayers.

"I have found it extraordinarily hard to talk to God," I wrote in my journal during a particularly dark spell. "As all vestiges of guaranteed Christian happiness have drained away, I have found little confidence that Christ even listens to me. So it's hard to press in. It's hard to invest any time into talking to a person who may or may not give a damn about what I have to say."

For months I didn't want to use the *D* word. I fought it, because it felt like death to me, the death of everything. But eventually, I had to admit it to myself in my journal. I had to call it what it was: *Doubt*. I was no longer very sure of what I believed. I was a doubter. That might not sound like a crisis to everyone, but as someone who built faith on the foundation of certainty, it shook me to my core.

Doubt seemed to me like the point of no return, the beginning of the end. If I couldn't be sure of everything, it was only a matter of time before I couldn't be sure of anything. An endless stream of Christians was already throwing in the towel on their faith. If I owned up to my own skepticism, wasn't it a slippery slope to doing the same? And what would I be then? I had followed Jesus for as long as I could remember being alive. I couldn't recall a time when I didn't already love him. What would be left of me if that went away? How would I go on in life? My degree was in ministry. My experience was in teaching the Bible and writing about spiritual things. If my faith died, would I have to recant? How would I provide for my family?

Doubt might not be the unforgivable sin, but it felt like the un-confessable one. So I told no one. I squeezed my eyes shut and tried with all my might to keep believing. "I do believe in Jesus. I do . . . I . . ."

THE REALITY OF DOUBT

Doubt is a fear-filled word for many of us. We were introduced to doubt as the sworn enemy of faith. So naturally, we built up defenses against questions that could leave us vulnerable. We readied ourselves to give an answer to the hope we professed.

Still, questions have a way of penetrating our defenses: Is God really there? Does God really love us? Is the Bible actually true?

Jason's doubts came by way of grief, but they come in other doors too. They come from rejection and betrayal, from reading books we weren't supposed to read or talking to people we weren't supposed to like. However they get past our barriers, once these questions take root, they begin to multiply like weeds. We pull one up only to find three more, and, before we know it, we are not convinced of anything at all. Back in the second stage, Confident Faith, the solution was to vigilantly ensure no such doubts were ever planted in the soil of our hearts and minds. But now there are legions of them. How do we grow if we are forced to silence every question?

The panic that comes with watching your belief in God wither before your eyes is traumatic, and not easily forgotten.

But we'll let you in on a little secret: doubt is a fairly universal human experience. Almost every person's emotional and intellectual palette includes doubt—even people of faith, even the most stalwart of saints. If we want our faith to survive this onslaught, we're going to have to change our attitude toward doubt.

Mother Teresa, whose name is synonymous with lifelong, active faithfulness, advised seekers to "love until it hurts," advice she herself famously lived out to the full. But this did not rid her of questions. Rather, Mother Teresa experienced profound doubts nearly all her life. Sometimes she wondered if God even existed. She wrote in a letter:

> Where is my faith? Even deep down . . . there is nothing but emptiness and darkness. . . . If there be God—please forgive me. When I try to raise my thoughts to Heaven, there is such convicting emptiness that those very thoughts return like sharp knives and hurt my very soul.[2]

Friend, do you hear, do you recognize the anguish in those words? Have you felt these words in your own soul? Have you buried your questions, worried that doubts are dirty and shameful, unfit for a people nicknamed Believers?

Consider the ancient Hebrews, who quickly tired of following a cloud through the wilderness for decades. Who wouldn't? It doesn't surprise us that, after their leader disappeared for several weeks, they pooled their resources and built a god they could understand, a statue they could hold in their hands, an idol who would keep them safe as long as they did what they were told.[3]

Sounds like a pretty sweet deal, actually.

But astonishingly, God was inviting them—and us—to something better. Not a rock-solid formula, but trust, an invitation to follow, to keep walking into relationship and mystery with a God they (and we) could not control. To believe he was good amid decades of detours and struggle. To believe he was faithful, never leaving, always beside them—even though life was brutally hard, even when they themselves proved disappointing and faithless. They didn't have visual guarantees. Unlike their neighbors and contemporaries, they couldn't see God with their eyes or hold God in their hands: that was the whole deal, the promise and the problem. They had to keep walking forward in faith, even when they could see nothing—even amid the assailing clouds of doubt and confusion.

This grasping, this stumbling in the dark? That's real. That's where we all are, truth be told, whether we know it or not.

In C. S. Lewis's *The Silver Chair*, Puddleglum the Marshwiggle is the eternal pessimist, never able to muster a single thread of hope that even one thing will go his way. But he stays the course, never leaves his post. And when the heroes of the story have been bewitched into believing Aslan does not exist, that their own good and lovely world was never true, it is Puddleglum who breaks the enchantment by insisting that even so merely the idea of Aslan, and sunshine, and home was compelling enough that he was going to live that story, even if nothing came of it.[4]

Like Puddleglum, we both find one question awaiting us each time we fall into the abyss of doubts: Am I fully convinced—about anything? The answer has been no. At least not all the time, not very often.

But is the story of a loving God who sees us—who is present even in our weakest, most broken moments, who is committed to a long, slow process of making all creation new and right—a sufficiently compelling story for me to step into, and stumble around in, even so? Yes. For us, at least most of the time, the answer is yes.

We're happy to report that this story, this faith, does not require us to exhaust ourselves to hold it up. It does not need vigilant defending. Instead, this faith holds *us* up, keeps us pointed forward as we walk through the wilderness.

That high-pressure "Tinkerbell faith" wasn't faith at all. It was a magic system. We don't have to keep believing really, really hard at all times without wavering in order to keep God alive. If your confidence has felt like that, and you can no longer keep it from crumbling . . . maybe it's best to let it go.

LETTING GO

When I (Jason) finally worked up the nerve to confess my secret doubts to someone, I chose my spiritual director—a retired pastor named Jeff. I had met with him off and on for a few years, and I knew he wouldn't shrink back from me in horror.

It was a messy conversation. I told him I was tired of holding onto faith in the middle of darkness. I talked about the old days when my belief was obvious and came easily. I felt spiritually invincible back then. God had seemed so real, and the planks of my Christian foundation were set with such tight precision there was no room for doubt. I had been sure of my faith. I had been *convinced*.

The memory sent an ache through my body. "I miss certainty," I said at last.

Before I spoke this out loud, I didn't realize how central those words were to understanding my crisis. I had grown up with an addiction to certainty, and now I was going through withdrawal. I didn't know how to understand a faith that could mingle openly with doubts, that didn't need to be firmly cemented in dogmatism.

Anne Lamott put a finer point on it. "The opposite of faith is not doubt, but certainty. Certainty is missing the point entirely. Faith includes noticing the mess, the emptiness and discomfort, and letting it be there until some light returns."[5]

Truth be told, we are almost never certain about anything. Every day, we make calculated decisions based on the evidence at hand. The bus might not arrive at 8:45 a.m. Our boss might extend that hard-and-fast deadline. The partly cloudy skies might turn into a thunderstorm, and all our party planning will be for nothing. And yet, we go about our lives.

The stakes are higher when it comes to relationships. We make wedding vows, take job offers, and add babies to our families—but we can't know with certainty what impact these people will have on our lives. Yet, we have to move forward. We have to live. So we choose a path that seems worthwhile, and we begin.

The most famous doubter of all time—the disciple Thomas— wanted assurances just like I do. He had heard the testimony of Jesus' resurrection but was not convinced. It was only when

Jesus himself showed up, alive, inviting him to touch his wounds, that Thomas was satisfied.

Jesus responded, "Because you have seen me, you have believed; blessed are those who have not seen and yet have believed" (John 20:29).

The more I consider this story, the more I am struck by it. Thomas wanted certainty, and in this case, he got it. But Jesus called blessed those who believe without seeing. Because, after all, that's what faith is. "Who hopes for what they already have?" Paul asked (Romans 8:24). When we see, we have no need to believe.

In Thomas's moment of revelation, he didn't need faith. He got his answer through sight and touch. He got his certainty. But for those of us still bumbling around without, we seek strength in what we do have, incomplete as it may be.

Right after Jesus' encounter with Thomas, John tells us this: "Jesus performed many other signs in the presence of his disciples, which are not recorded in this book. But these are written that you may believe that Jesus is the Messiah, the Son of God, and that by believing you may have life in his name" (John 20:30-31). Can you imagine all the stories of Jesus on earth that we'll never hear? But what we have been given is sufficient. Not for certainty, but for confidence. For faith.

One day, there will be no use for faith, for when everything is seen, then nothing will be unseen. There will be no need for brave determination to lean into the unknown. We will see not through a cloudy glass, but face to face.

This is what I longed for the day I sat with Jeff. I wanted the kind of resolution that would erase the need to keep on trusting Jesus—a once-for-all assurance that no tragedy could shake. I wanted to go back to the days of youthful self-delusion, when I had amassed a proud arsenal of untested answers. But I knew it was too late. I had to let it go.

There is no going back. I had two choices: ditch my belief in God or find a better definition of faith—one that didn't rely so much on me.

REFRAMING FAITH

The biblical concept of faith is different from the Tinkerbell faith we're quite ready to leave behind. When Jesus walked the earth, the default assumption for humans around the globe was that God (or gods) existed and evidence of their activity could be seen every day. Having faith wasn't about believing an invisible spirit was real or powerful; that was a given. Having faith was trusting that Jesus, Jesus' teachings, and Jesus' vision of a compassionate, forgiving, death-defeating God were compelling enough that we would band together and live life differently in light of these promises. That we would follow. That we would put our feet, and therefore our body, on the same path Jesus and his followers were on—and start walking along it wherever he went and whatever it cost.

In other words, the biblical idea of faith is *relational*. That's where the word *faithfulness* comes from, the quality of remaining in relationship in a trustworthy, ongoing way. There is a component of believing something to be true—any relationship requires belief in the other person to exist and to be worth investing in—but faith is primarily a relational way of life between God and us, and between Christ-followers as a community. We commit to traveling a path together, to heading in a direction together. That's where choice, decision, and even conviction come in—just not certainty.

This is good news for us doubters, for those of us who can no longer keep Tinkerbell's light on by believing hard enough. A vegetarian doesn't need to screw her eyes shut and clench her fists tight to believe in vegetarianism. She doesn't even need to think this is the only right path, or to feel unwavering emotions about it. A pacifist doesn't need to constantly visualize the lives saved or lost or hold strong feelings of grief or victory each day. What each needs is to have a conviction that this path is valuable to pursue, put research and thought behind it, then commit to the practice—ideally with a community of people who can ease the sacrifices and multiply the joys.

Granted, faith is further reaching and more transcendent than habits of eating and conflict resolution. There is the character of God to consider, and the many aspects of our lives we are asked to submit or change as we pursue a life with God. Questions still loom before us, such as, How do we commit to a relational path when we're not sure we can trust God or God's people? We'll look honestly at these in the chapters ahead. But for now, it's important to understand this groundwork: our faith is not something unbelievable we're trying hard to convince ourselves of but convictions in which we invest our time and energy. Faith is a destination mixed up with our dreams and hopes and desires, one that we would give our lives to—perhaps even our deaths. It's a vision of God's love, acceptance, and justice for the world, for ourselves. It's the story that motivates and drives us most powerfully, the path we find ourselves most consistently walking, the shape of the longings we can hardly speak aloud. It's the one thing we choose above all else. The story we most want to be true.

Do these things come with solid convictions and unwavering feelings? Probably not. Maybe, at certain times. But most days we are simply walking the path, or on the path unmoving, or even considering what it might look like to go elsewhere. But on the path still.

In the churches we both grew up in, liturgy or rote prewritten prayers got a hard rap. Prayer and expressions of faith needed to be from the heart. The more raw, the more emotional, the better. But this places such a heavy burden on the worshiper, the faith-practicer. Both of us have now found a degree of freedom in gathering in church buildings where the words of our faith are spoken all around us, whether or not we can join in ourselves at that very moment. Simply by standing in that room, with that community, before God, our bodies are saying, "I'm here. My feet are here. I've chosen this practice, this faith, because it's what I want and what I think is valuable. This is the story I choose."

EMBRACING THE STORY

"I was preparing a sermon last week," I told Jeff, staring at the dancing flames of the tabletop fireplace. "And while I was writing it, I wasn't even sure I believed it." I shuddered at the memory. I had felt like such a hypocrite.

I continued. "When I got up to preach, I felt the rush of conviction come back, but still, it scared me. I'm a pastor. What if my confidence level is only at, like, 50 percent on a given day? How much faith is enough for it to be real?"

Jeff loves to give long, uncomfortable pauses, because he knows silence has a way of flushing out the truth. But this time, he left no pause. Instead, he gave a little shrug and said words that changed my life: "Well, Jason, a mustard seed isn't very much."

I blinked back tears as I took in the thought. A mustard seed. It was a clear allusion to Jesus' words: "If you have faith as small as a mustard seed, you can say to this mountain, 'Move from here to there,' and it will move" (Matthew 17:20). I had always heard those words used to reference the miraculous power of faith itself, but not the minimal requirements of conviction. A mustard seed is small. Jesus was saying not only that faith is powerful but that a little goes a long way. And a little was all I had.

Could a person doubt and still walk in faith? The prospect made me sit up straight. I thought of the man who asked Jesus to heal his sick child. "I do believe," he said; "help my unbelief!" (Mark 9:24 NASB). That was me. And that was okay.

Jeff's words didn't dispel my doubt, but they did free me of my fear of doubt. I realized I no longer had to shut my eyes and grind my teeth, whispering, "I do believe in Jesus! I do! I do!" What was the point in that? Would it make Jesus any more or less real? Could I create or erase God by simply having a bad day?

Sometimes, I am still stirred up with spiritual fervor. When I visit the Oregon coast, I watch the everlasting waves beat against the jagged cliffs and listen to the birds sing of the One who made them fly—and my spirit soars with them. When I gather with friends and family to worship, I watch my own sons lift their hands to Jesus and my eyes fill with tears of gratitude and hope. On those days, my heart is delighted by the beauty I find in God's story, in Jesus' good news, in a life intentionally angled toward devotion and wonder.

On other days, when the fog of uncertainty sets in and I cannot see the sun through all my pain, I don't have to grind my teeth and channel my pompous, eighteen-year-old self anymore. I can simply hold the tiny mustard seed, and keep on going.

WHERE DO WE GO FROM HERE?

The book of John tells of a day when many of Jesus' followers began to abandon him. It was a sobering moment. Jesus looked at his disciples and asked if they, too, would walk away. Peter answered. "Lord, to whom shall we go? You have the words of eternal life" (John 6:68).

There is no hint of Peter's typical bravado in that answer. Only simple honesty. There was no place else to go but onward.

The fact that Jesus would accept, no delight, in the faith of doubters like Peter and Thomas, Catherine and Jason—that is good news for those who are poor and hungry, lost and wandering, for those who might not be certain all the time but who still find the story of Jesus to be the greatest one ever told. We have no place else to go. Since there is no path named Certainty, we choose the one named Faith. And somehow, it is enough.

This is how Mother Teresa dealt with her doubts: she decided the story of Jesus was the pearl of greatest price. With her life, she emulated Jesus, investing her desires and hopes, time and energy, mind and body into the work she believed was God's kingdom on earth—the kingdom where those who weep are comforted, where the poor are provided for, the sick are healed, and the prisoners released. Where justice and goodness pour over the entire world like a mighty flowing stream.

And this is what keeps us going too, amid hopes and doubts and convictions and questions. The world where God's goodness, mercy, love, and justice have overcome all our efforts toward destruction, hate, suffering, and oppression is a world we want to invest in. And for the two of us, the days when we live as if God's story is real are the days we feel most vividly alive.

It might be hard to believe Jesus' vision for God's kingdom, hard to believe that compassion and mercy will have the final word. It might be hard to believe that God is good some days, that God is love. And that's okay. It's okay if your faith feels small right now. All you need to have is a mustard seed. All you need to do is lay it on the ground and trust that it will grow.

This is the practice of faith.

PRACTICE

⸽⸽⸽ *Redefining Faith*

If you, too, learned to define faith as believing in full certainty without wavering, your mid-faith crisis may involve struggles with doubt as ours did. Learning to view faith as a trajectory you choose with conviction and hope may be a helpful way to move forward. Here are a few practical steps that might help in the process.

- Set aside time to consider beliefs you once held with certainty (or believed you ought to hold with certainty) that you now question or doubt. Consider writing these down, talking with a trusted friend (or spiritual director or other professional as Jason did), or in some other way moving them from your thoughts to outside of your body. Create enough safe space for yourself that you can honestly sift through your thoughts and allow surprises to come to mind.

- Make a list of convictions you hold, yearnings you long for, visions you have for the world or for yourself. Include rituals, traditions, disciplines, and practices that are important to you. Examples may include traditional spiritual or religious activities or may be quite different, such as goals for travel, relationships, social change, or dietary choices. In other words, what matters to you? What do you value enough to invest time and effort into cultivating? Then consider the ways you are committed to a long-term pursuit of these things, regardless of your feelings from day to day. In what ways is this process similar to the life of faith? To what degree do you choose to include a life of faith in this list?

- Find a tiny seed and hold it in your hand. (You may be able to find one outside, but if not, look in a garden supply department . . . or even your spice cupboard!) Consider how small your seed is, how forgettable and weak it appears, how easily swept away and lost. Now, consider what it has the capacity to grow into, if the conditions are right. In what way is faith like this? Give your seed to God in some way: toss it into the air, or lay it on the ground. Or, take a packet of seeds and place it somewhere to remind yourself that you are choosing the journey of faith and this tiny start is all that you need.
- Sit or walk quietly, slowly echoing the prayer of the father in Mark 9:23-25 (NASB). "Lord, I believe. Help my unbelief." Pray the first line as you breathe in and the second line as you breathe out. Pause between breaths, then repeat.

Something to Listen To

- "Jesus, I Have My Doubts," Jon Foreman
- "Rescue Me," The Brilliance

Something to Read

- *After Doubt: How to Question Your Faith Without Losing It*, A.J. Swoboda
- *When Everything's on Fire: Faith Forged from the Ashes*, Brian Zahnd

4

WHEN CHURCH WAS HARMFUL

To me the Wisconsin farming town I (Catherine) grew up in felt larger than life. From the ancient water tower at one end to the expansive forested park at the other, I knew every road like the back of my hand. The Tastee Freez we biked to for ice cream cones served the best soft-serve (chocolate dipped) I could imagine. The tiny library held old musty books, and the equally musty theater played second-run films, but each was my portal to the universe. My first definition of freedom was walking with my brother to the Ben Franklin dime store downtown and coming home with a full fifty cents worth of candy.

My memories began here. This was home in the way only a small community you were born into can be. It was the most important place on the planet.

So, when my pastor-dad was fired from the church he had served, when they decided to erase our family rather than allow us to transition, it didn't just affect employment. It took away my world. What would have been a major but survivable destabilization in a different line of work (or a

more compassionate church) turned into layers of upheaval
for us.

Those days were awful, but I don't really remember them.
What can you remember about such a short and terrible time,
in which you lose everything and everyone?

A few moments stand out. The recital I'd worked toward for
months was scheduled during that time, and when my mom
called for the details, she was told I was no longer invited to
perform. Everyone felt it would be best for my family to keep
out of sight until we had left for good. I was twelve years old,
and I was uninvited from my own piano recital.

During my final week at the only school I had ever attended,
I wrote up a will and asked my friends what items of mine they
wanted in the event of my early death. At the time, this felt like
a silly way to say goodbye. Looking back at it now, I realize
how poignant this game was: I knew I was severing both from
the people I knew and loved and from the tangible components of the only world I knew. What was this, if not a death?

As my classmates divvied up (in theory) my books and
stickers and trendiest pencils, one of my teachers saw through
the game. He gently responded, "Catherine, I don't want anything. You just stay alive." I remember this so vividly because
it was the only message I heard during that time—or would
hear for a long time—that said, "I see you. I have compassion
for you. You are suffering, and I want you to survive."

But that was it. We left town when the two weeks were up.
We were not invited to come back or keep in touch. With my
parents' careers and marriage both in shreds, there was no easy
way to start over. We packed up the car and arrived almost

without warning to my dad's brother's basement a few states away, like refugees.

WHEN THE CHURCH FAILS

Most stories we hear of church hurt involve pastors abusing authority. This has happened for eons, and we see it so often now that it's almost become a cliché. But sometimes the story is a bit different: it's a Sunday school volunteer, a prominent teacher or powerhouse family in the church, or a holy keyboard warrior who wields God's name to harm others. When someone holds authority—especially spiritual authority—the damage that person can inflict is almost unlimited. The temptation to turn our faith communities and practices into expressions of power rather than Christlikeness is strong and common, and has catastrophic effects.

For many of us, our primary and longest lasting faith crisis was sparked by the utter failure of the church—locally or globally—to be like Christ, to protect the vulnerable, to show compassion, to reject the temptations of wealth and power and stand against oppressors and oppression. In this way, Catherine's story is as common as the sun rising; every day we encounter someone who trusted, who believed they were safe in their community of faith, only to find that they were anything but.

The How It Started vs. How It's Going photos for this kind of crisis look especially grim. In the first picture we find (what we believe to be) healthy community, safety, belonging, and protection. We can trust these people. We're at home here with them. We choose vulnerability and cultivate a spiritual posture of surrender because we believe we are in a safe and nurturing place, a place where God—the good and loving Creator and Savior—is present and glorified. Truly, this is what the church is meant to be, what family and community are intended to provide, and it is within these imperfect-but-loving arms that we humans are able to become, to discover who we are and grow to take our own place in the community. A spiritual community can powerfully name us and call us forth, shaping who we are in every respect—and keep us steadily faithful for a lifetime.

But when imperfect crosses the line into toxic, abusive, controlling, or manipulative, great harm is done, for that same power can misshape and destroy. The second photo in this collage is one of total disaster—spiritually as well as emotionally, mentally, socially, even physically. Words like "egregious violation of trust" fit here. Abuse. Manipulation. Neglect. #ChurchToo.

Then, too often, those who cry for help are told that they are the problem, that the church family's dirty laundry should not be displayed for all the world to see. That the ministry must be protected at all costs.

The ones who suffer are too often ignored and left out in the cold. Their fallout has only just begun.

THE FALLOUT

The next ten years of my (Catherine's) life were hard, every single one, in every possible way. Our problems doubled and doubled again, as nearly always happens to destabilized people. For a time, we were essentially homeless. After a few months

in my uncle's basement, we moved into a house too uninhab-
itable to be legally rented. During these years—from before we
left "home" until several years after—my dad had cancer
growing in his body but no money or insurance to have it re-
moved. Like most people trying to survive, he followed the
only path he could: just live with it. And so he did, and almost
died with it too.

I turned thirteen and moved from school to school. I felt
alone and unknown. I never, ever, ever told anybody how we
came to be where we were, who we were. No one who knew us
before ever, ever talked to me about what happened. Without
a way to go back, without an ongoing relationship with the
community of my childhood, I had no way to create a bridge
from who I had been and who I was. There was then, and there
was now. Before, After. Every detail of my life changed, even
the silly little ones. But they create an identity, bit by bit.

- Before: unpasteurized whole milk straight from the cow
- After: skim milk from the convenience store

- Before: regular soda
- After: diet soda

- Before: long hair and skirts
- After: short hair and jeans

- Before: fundamentalist Christian school
- After: secular public school

- Before: perfect pastor's kid
- After: messed-up life in every way

Most troubling (and impactful long term) of all, these years were hard because it was vividly clear to me that I had lost everything and everyone because we were unworthy of being known and loved, of being kept. They had kicked us out. I had been abandoned not by one person but by everyone I knew in the world. It thoroughly broke me to discover so viscerally that my family and I were so worthy of rejection by everyone—by my home, church, school, family, everyone I knew—so deeply rejected that we were dead to them. Dead to everyone I had known. Without compassionate adults who knew my story, there was no way for me to process what had happened and was still happening, no way for me to hear a different narrative.

For a long time, I was so, so angry and hurt. Broken into pieces. So very untrusting. So vigilant, for in addition to the upheaval of the past and present there was this question: What else might happen to end the world?

To say my childhood church's treatment of my family impacted my faith in God, my relationship with the church and with Christians, and my understanding of Christianity is a huge understatement. I powerfully deconstructed before I entered puberty, and long before there was a word to describe it. It is hard to accept anything—relational or doctrinal—from a group of people who cast you out when you were a child and made it abundantly clear you were not allowed back.

I don't think I made a conscious decision to stop going to church. My body took over and provided the safety my first-born, people-pleasing temperament could not intentionally choose for myself. When my family settled down enough to start attending a new congregation, I started becoming physically ill every Sunday morning. So, I stayed home and made mixtapes instead, listening to the *American Top 40* countdown with my old-school cassette player hooked up to a mic pointed at the radio speakers. "Church" had been my whole world, where I had found love and home, friends and family, meaning and identity, even school. And "church" had tossed me out, declared me too unlovable to even check and see if I'd survived.

GATEKEEPERS

Stage three faith will always feel like a wilderness, but never more so than when one has tasted betrayal and been sent packing. The double-edged sword of the church-abuse-flavored mid-faith crisis is that this pushes people out of community and leaves them to suffer alone. Some people, like Catherine, are literally exiled out of community. Others realize they have no choice but to leave it all behind. Most struggle to trust a new Christian community ever again. This is a recipe for compounding disaster. But what can you do when you've been mistreated, or even sent away?

If there is a blessing in this kind of hurt, it is simply this: separation from the ones who inflicted harm is often the first step toward healing. When there has been a misuse of authority—that is, when those who are powerful inflict harm on those in their care—there is no easy way to reconcile. Sometimes the abuse victims or their advocates try to sound the alarm and bring attention to the destruction taking place. But too often they are redirected to a private, one-on-one meeting with the very person or group misusing power, thanks to a misapplication of Matthew 18. Those one-on-one confrontations prove utterly disastrous of course: a victim of sexual abuse (for example) trying to confront their pastor will experience even more intense intimidation and harm. If the balance of power has been exploited and the compassion of Christlike relationships overturned, only further destruction will result from sending a victim back to his or her abuser in private.

This is no time for "a friendly chat." Evoking Matthew 18 in abuse situations ignores both the context of the passage and the situation at hand. In Matthew 18, Jesus was addressing his disciples, who knew one another as equals: Peter and John, Andrew and James, Thomas and Bartholomew. He was addressing a group of friends who worked together on the same level. He wasn't speaking to a mixed group of religious leaders and the people they had broken. Jesus had plenty of direct words to say to religious leaders who abused their power and harmed their sheep, and these words were quite different.

The Gospel of John tells of a man who suffered this kind of hurt on what should have been the greatest day of his life (John 9). The man had been born blind and left to beg outside the temple for his daily bread. Indeed, he had done this for so long that he had become something of a staple. People in Jerusalem knew this guy. They had all tiptoed around him at least once.

But Jesus went straight to him and did something strange. He shoved mud in the man's eyes and told him to go wash. The man obeyed, and when his eyes were clear, he could see. He returned to his spot—and was met not with rejoicing but with anger.

The religious leaders were furious with him. Why? Because he told them the truth: it was Jesus who had done it. Rather than celebrating the man's good fortune, they sensed that their own power over the people was threatened. When he wouldn't recant his testimony, they did the unthinkable: they exiled him. They threw him out of the synagogue.

For this man who had survived years of suffering, the synagogue was as large and prominent as Catherine's childhood church. It was the center of community, the source of spiritual life, truth, and belonging. The synagogue was everything.

Is it possible that, in that moment, he resented his healing? Is having eyesight truly better than having a home, a place to belong? The hurt and shock he felt at being turned out must have been immense and acute. Excommunicated for the crime of being healed? Of encountering God's compassion made flesh (and deeply contrasted to this earthly way of leading)? Incredible.

But watch what happened next, because it's easy to miss: Jesus resurfaced, and he did not act as you might expect. He did not tell the man to go and reconcile with his leaders. He did not tell him to find common ground, or to have a larger discussion with more leaders. No. Rather, Jesus saw the situation and saw the man who had been shut out, and told him, "I am the door" (John 10:9 KJV). *Jesus is the door.*

In other words, the religious leaders who hurt the man were not the real gatekeepers. The skeptics who refused to believe his story didn't hold the keys to faith and healing. Only Christ holds those keys. He opens the gate to acceptance and love. He holds the keys to life and life abundantly. He is the door.

For those who have been shut out, or pushed out, this is good news. Jesus is the door.

Jesus was not talking quietly. Everyone could hear him, and he knew it. He talked about the cruelty of spiritual shepherds who come like thieves to steal, kill, and destroy. The entire speech is a reference to an old, angry prophecy from the book of Ezekiel (Ezekiel 34:1-31), which excoriates the cruelty of religious shepherds who abuse their sheep. Jesus was not so subtly and oh so publicly confronting leaders who had just wounded the man born blind. "This is you," Jesus is telling them. "And I'm not going to stand for it."

In contrast, he says, "I am the good shepherd," and "I am come that they might have life, and that they might have it more abundantly" (John 10:11, 10 KJV).

Friend, if you've been hurt by your religious community, if you've been turned out by command or by circumstance, you need to know this: Jesus sits outside with you. Jesus is the Good Shepherd who seeks out the little ones, the forgotten ones, the one sheep who is lost and alone. Jesus champions the oppressed and is near to the brokenhearted. The evil shepherds who locked you out do not have the power to shut you out from the love of God or life in the Spirit.

If anything, you who feel so unseen and alone, you are the one Jesus is caring for most, now.

"IT'S COMPLICATED"

The only thing more real and certain to me than the trauma I (Catherine) experienced at the hands of the church is the slow, gentle work of God's healing presence in my life. But it took long, long years and more before I could even begin to see it.

When I entered college, this new season in a new place felt like a chance at rebirth, a way to learn who I was outside of my family and the weight of our narrative. This was a gift, an invitation to open myself up intellectually, spiritually, relationally. For the first time, I started dabbling in real friendship. I remember being stunned one day when a new friend actually stood up for me. Why would she choose me at the expense of other relationships? I thought. Why would anyone choose me? That was when I finally found the courage to tell my story for the first time. I did it little by little, one friend at a time.

In this slow way, I allowed myself to be cracked open, not only by human friends but by God, who began coaxing me out of my protective shell. At first, I kicked and screamed in response to that coaxing. But God was so vividly in front of me, like a cloud by day and a fire by night, pointing me forward. I at last began to yield. To come out of my hiding place.

There were moments—fleeting ones, but miraculous, life-changing ones—when God even convinced me he had been with me all along. God showed up for me vividly, with pictures I could see in my imagination, with words in my head that seemed to come out of nowhere. I remember one night in particular when I held years of devastating pain and stubborn hatred in my hands and heard God ask me to let go of it, to set it down and let him replace it with forgiveness. I don't have words to express how hard I fought that night. But I surrendered eventually and began the long walk toward restoration.

In some ways, I'm still on that journey. It's been over thirty years since my world was ripped away from me. I have done a lot of work. I've been to therapy and required myself to take relational risks and relearn a bit of trust. Even though my emotional wounds are healing, the scars remain.

And church? Well, as they say, "It's complicated." I've invested my adult life in church communities—I'm even finishing up an MDiv as I write this book, to better serve the church in the future. But I don't do this lightly. While I no longer spend my Sunday mornings making mixtapes, I've never again felt fully included or safe within a church. I know deeply that every community and movement—including churches—is full of broken people, hurting people, including both predators and those they devour. I have peered into the dark rooms and forgotten corners, and there are no questions I fear asking or holding; I hold no illusions at all anymore. This in itself gives me a degree of freedom and an invitation to beauty and truth. It allows me to walk alongside others as they question and grieve.

I take nothing at face value or expect a person's veneer to show the whole story. I am neither impressed by charismatic leaders nor easily persuaded to find wisdom in a passionate sermon. I am grateful to see acts of genuine compassion when I encounter them, but I am never shocked by scandals. I don't get swayed by platform or flash, and I always want to peer beneath the surface before passing judgment. I never forget that there's a whole person waiting beneath every façade.

In one very tangible step toward healing years ago, I drove my now-husband to the town where this all happened. I was stunned by how very normal it was. To my absolute shock, this small community in the middle of Wisconsin farmland didn't look at all like the all-powerful center of the universe I thought it was. It was simply one more nondescript exit off the highway like any other town. I drove Matthew all around, seeing everything, going everywhere—places I still remembered clearly since they had buried themselves so deeply inside of me. I didn't tell anyone I was coming or that I was there. Arriving like this and leaving again on my own terms felt like taking some power back. You can't send someone away if she can drive her own car back any time she wants to.

When I drove away that day, I tried to leave it all behind. This place had made an indelible mark on my soul, but I no longer gave it the power to name my identity, speak for God, or define my faith.

THE COURAGE TO HEAL

In Catherine's story, there could be no real reconciliation with the community that hurt her. Too many years had passed, and too much had changed. When she did finally go back, she did it on her terms and in her own timing, for her own reasons.

Going back is never as easy as outsiders like to tell us it is. Reconciliation is simply not always possible. For many people, the hurt is too great, especially for those who have experienced abuse. When a shepherd or a church devours its own, those sheep cannot find safety, peace, or belonging—let alone reconciliation or the goodness of God—in the same setting or even a similar one. A new group of people isn't always enough. Sometimes you need an entirely new scene in a different town.

Or, like Catherine, you might need to take a break from church for a while. In the religious status of your online profiles, you might need to select, "It's complicated." That's okay. Healing requires a measure of space and time. God isn't often, if ever, in a hurry.

Maybe you will never feel comfortable inside the walls of a church again. That's a painful reality we can't ignore. Thankfully, God exists beyond the walls we build. You can find him in the coffee shop, in a stroll by the river, or around the dinner table of a trusted friend. You might even find him on the airwaves of top-40 radio.

Whether or not you ever find your way back to church, we hope you will at least find a path back to some sort of healthy community. Even though it's hard, even though not everyone can choose this, if and when you can, we think the best route to full healing is in a community of people who can (imperfectly) emulate Jesus, binding up the wounds left by those who hurt you.

Regardless of when and how you find healing, you will need courage. Catherine's healing took hold only after she slowly began to share her story with a trusted community—and for someone who has been abused or abandoned, this can feel (and be) so very risky. When she spoke the truth that was buried at the center of her soul, the fear and pain began to lose its grip, bit by bit. We are relational beings, and we were made for community.

And that's not fair, for it was community that wounded us in the first place. But if we may be so bold to say: The ones who abused you do not speak for Jesus; they do not represent God.

They never had that authority. While the impact of their actions may be the largest and most powerful thing in your life, that place is not the epicenter of truth. In fact, the church community that hurt you in the name of Jesus was but a small town off the highway that is Christianity. Jesus sits with the outsiders, the lost and wandering ones. He is near to the brokenhearted. He is the door.

Yes, other shepherds have the power to wound us, deeply. But they do not have the right to name you.

Years ago, my wife and I (Jason) left our home in California without knowing what would come next. As we left our work with an international missions agency, we came to a small town near Eugene, Oregon. We had a relationship with a church there, and they had invited us to come rest for a month as we figured out our next move. I had never felt so weak in my life. I was still grieving the loss of a close friend and the diagnosis of my son Jack. I was beaten down and thoroughly depressed by the prospect of never knowing my son.

We ended up staying for a year, settling down in the community while we tried to work through our family trauma. In that season of brokenness, the church suddenly and unexpectedly offered me a job as the new associate pastor. I was utterly baffled. When I went into the Tuesday morning elders' meeting to discuss the offer, I tried to talk them out of it.

"I don't think you guys understand what you're getting into," I said. "I'm at the weakest point in my entire life. I don't know if I can do this. I don't know what I even have to offer right now."

I'll never forget their kind smiles and small shoulder shrugs. They knew all about my brokenness. For the past year, they had walked with our family. They had surrounded us, prayed with us, let us cry on their shoulders. They had watched me fall on my face in complete failure, and helped me get up and make things right.

"We will do this together," they told me. "Don't worry. We won't let you fall."

They were true to their word. Fourteen years later, we are still here, with these same people. They never gave up on me. They haven't let me fall.

We have shared countless meals over countless tables and shared the stories that defined us. We have celebrated marriages and mourned separations, welcomed newborn children and committed the dying to God. Through this community, we've felt the Good Shepherd walking alongside us. Through their kindness, we've felt the presence of Jesus, opening the door to let us grieve and to let us heal, as often as we've needed.

We "go to church" on Sundays for corporate worship, but we also have church in our backyards, around firepits, and at the Oregon coast. Church is not a building, a business, or a territory. The church is people. And it's in those quieter, more organic settings that our souls find the most rest.

These folks aren't perfect, and neither am I. We hurt each other, sometimes. We let each other down, fail to be sensitive, disappoint one another. But these things happen to the normal degree, in the brothers-and-sisters-who-love-each-other kind of way. We aren't perfect, but we aren't abusive or misusing power. So, because abuse is absent, love really does cover a multitude of sins (1 Peter 4:8).

I know not everyone will have this experience. Not everyone finds this kind of warmth. We too are, after all, just one small town off another forgotten exit on the church highway. But there are communities of faith in the world who don't just speak about Jesus: they resemble Jesus. It is in their company that I have most clearly felt the goodness of God.

AFTER ALL THIS

Like the unpasteurized milk and long skirts of my (Catherine's) dairy-farming childhood, there's very little left of my faith from "before." Everything I have now, I wrestled over and fought for in the "after." My faith was built atop all this, after all this, with the knowledge of all this. My faith exists at all because God met me in suffering and doubt. What else is there to be threatened by?

One of my favorite songs is "Goodness of God." Every word feels true to me.

> You have led me through the fire
> And in darkest night, you are close like no other. . . .
> With every breath that I am able,
> I will sing of the goodness of God.[1]

Of course, it did not feel that way at the time. It did not feel that God was close, not for years after. But my testimony is that I am confident now that he is present always, even in the darkest night. If, after all this, I can genuinely say that God's goodness has been running after me—then I feel it must be true.

Friend, if your experience and faith crisis are anything like mine, I grieve that you were harmed by those who claimed to be the expression of God's love for you. And while I will never tell you to go back to those who abused you, I pray you will find people who deeply know you and allow you to know them in return, whose imperfections fall far, far short of exploitation and abuse—and that you can love them and be loved in return. I pray that you will join me, someday, eventually, in looking back and discovering that goodness has been running after you, all this time.

PRACTICE

|||||||||||||||||||||||||||||||||||||||||||||||||||||||||||||||| *Reimagining Safe Community*

If your mid-faith crisis was launched by harm done to you through the church, or in the name of Jesus, it's likely that you too struggle to find safety in community. If you have been separated from the people you called home, it will take time to remember that they were never the doorkeepers of God's kingdom, that Jesus himself is the door.

Take time to name what happened to you, and what you lost, and grieve that. Depending on where you are in your process, this may take a moment, or it may take years. You may be ready to move forward after a few moments of quiet reflection, or you may need to make an appointment with a therapist.

Using prayer, journaling, music, or art (to name just a few ideas), explore what you believed about the people who harmed you or let you down. What did they teach you (implicitly or explicitly) about yourself and your identity before

God? Which of these things are valuable and worth holding on to? Which of these things are harmful or outdated and need to be let go?

The practice of returning to community will look different during the stages of this process. Here are some questions that may help you find a path forward.

- Who are the people I can trust with my whole self?
- Do I feel safe and included in my current worshiping community?
- What would it look like to join, or rejoin, a Christian community? What would I need to believe this could be a move toward goodness, not brokenness? What are the signs that this community is imperfect but healthy versus dangerous and unhealthy?
- If committing to a church or Christian community sounds impossible to you, where can you gather with people who encourage you toward health and wholeness?
- Do you know others who have a similar need? How can you help each other, or how could the steps you take for yourself be extended to them?

Something to Listen To

- "Out of Hiding," Steffany Gretzinger
- "You'll Never Walk Alone," Aretha Franklin
- "Constellations," Ellie Holcomb

Something to Read

- *Healing Spiritual Wounds: Reconnecting with a Loving God After Experiencing a Hurtful Church*, Carol Howard Merritt
- *Searching for Sunday: Loving, Leaving, and Finding the Church*, Rachel Held Evans

- *A Church Called Tov: Forming a Goodness Culture That Resists Abuses of Power and Promotes Healing*, Scot McKnight and Laura McKnight Barringer
- *Restoring the Shattered Self: A Christian Counselor's Guide to Complex Trauma*, Heather Davediuk Gingrich

5

WHEN OUR HEROES FELL

"Have you heard of this guy, Ravi Zacharias?"

When I (Jason) was new in ministry, I knew little of the poetry of faith. To me, God was a God of order, and that's who I loved: the Lord and Lawgiver penning precepts on our hearts, even carving them onto tablets of stone once upon a time. I marveled at the Creator who made our minds and invited prophets to argue at his table. I drifted toward teachers and writers who leaned into rational apologetics of the Francis Schaeffer variety, people who could follow the divine logic "precept upon precept, line upon line" (Isaiah 28:10 KJV).

In the early 2000s, I discovered podcasts. Suddenly, I had choices. I could listen to the teachers I had always heard, or I could find new voices. And oh, did I find a voice!

When I first heard Ravi Zacharias speak, I was at once intrigued and addicted. I downloaded every episode of his nationally syndicated radio shows, *Just Thinking* and *Let My People Think*. In the evenings, I would wash dishes to the beat of his oratory. Through the cadence of his words, I began to adopt an entirely new outlook on faith and ministry. Yes, order and logic were gifts. But so was poetry, and Ravi wove the two together beautifully. The same Holy Spirit who gave the Torah to Moses inspired the Song of Solomon. The Great Engineer who wrote the laws of nature was the Great Artist who painted the night sky.

It was all so lovely. I never knew the gospel could sound like that.

Who are your heroes? We all have them, even if that's not a word we would think to use to describe them. Parents, teachers, older siblings, real-life adults, and larger-than-life stars of legends—we begin our journey through life by carefully placing our small feet in the big footprints our heroes leave behind.

Whether we came to faith as children or adults, we began our faith journey in the same way: picking our way behind those who came before us (whether they intended us to follow or not). The How It Started snapshot of our faith often shows our faces tilted, beaming hopefully in the direction of a man or woman who embodied everything we aspired to become: a godly teacher, a compelling pastor, a joy-filled devotee. We first understood what it could mean to look like Jesus by looking at them. We imagined the details of a faithful life well lived by considering their way in the world.

Our hearts were open and trusting in those early days. We were fertile ground, clay ready to be shaped. We need each other to be "Jesus with skin on" as they say, and we transferred the trust we placed in our loving and all-wise Creator into the fallible hands of mentors. This is natural, and necessary—and a sobering responsibility too. It's how we begin anything, how we learn.

Trouble is, humans are—well, human. Ideally, we learn to see through our heroes to the God they humbly if imperfectly reflect. Ideally, our heroes actively shrug off the capes we place on their shoulders and point the way to Jesus. But in our celebrity-shaped culture, that step often gets left out. We're taught to idolize our heroes to the point of worship, taught to grasp the mantle of influence as tightly as we can.

Then comes the crisis.

THE CRISIS

"Have you heard of this guy, Ravi Zacharias?" I (Jason) would ask. Most people hadn't. I filled them in: Ravi was the next Billy Graham. Born and raised in India, he became an evangelist in North America, giving him (what to my ears was) an irresistible accent along with an ability to expertly navigate questions of global philosophy and religion. Ravi was an evangelist for all hemispheres: east and west, heart and mind.

I cannot overstate the impact Ravi had on my formation. Though I never met him, he became my daily teacher and mentor. I developed a taste for real literature, works shot through with metaphor. I found my teaching style and depth changing as a result. I became a storyteller. I sought to emulate his cadence on stage, holding out my s's at the end of money quotes. When I began to write for publication, I would hear his voice narrating my words, making them sound warm, intelligent, and full of poetry. It seemed clear that apologists like

Ravi had the ammunition necessary to decimate any argument against the faith, yet they were gentle with atheists and those who debated them. They didn't feel the need to embarrass others. One of my old teachers used to say, "Truth is relaxed." I saw what that looked like in Ravi, and that gave me confidence. Sure, Richard Dawkins and Sam Harris had questions I couldn't answer. But now, I was certain, there *were* answers, and Ravi probably had them all.

When Ravi died of cancer in 2020, I felt such immense gratitude for his ministry that I posted on my Facebook page: "The greatest thing that Ravi taught me was that truth should be beautiful. #ThankYouRavi"

The truth, however, was far from beautiful.

The headlines came out months after his death. This man I revered had not been a man of God, but a sexual predator.[1] The allegations were staggering in their breadth: not a single incident or moment of weakness, not a fling or even an affair but something much worse—a lifestyle of premeditated sexual exploitation, abuse, and assault. The victims of his carefully constructed predatory behavior included women in his hometown and all over the world. In a breathtaking misuse of spiritual power, Ravi would tell them of the pressures in being "a man of God," then refer to the women as his "reward" for saving souls.[2]

I felt sick. How could the warm and wise grandfather who spoke of Jesus with heart-wrenching lyrical force be *this man*? It didn't make sense.

ANOTHER KIND OF CHURCH HURT

You've likely heard the phrase, commonly attributed to boxer Robert Fitzsimmons, "The bigger they come, the harder they fall." In our Western world, enamored by fantasies of upward mobility, of elevators to penthouse apartments and stars on stages, we've seen it over and over: the people we worship rise like titans to the sky, then crash down into a dumpster of indictments, secret lives, and #MeToo. It happens so often we almost expect it.

We'd be hard pressed to name a hero still considered above reproach. Recent scandals in the North American church have shaken us. From Hillsong to Mars Hill, from Gothard seminars to the Southern Baptist Convention, our heroes hit the ground like bad apples.[3] And as the saying goes, one bad apple spoils the whole barrel. Millions of us have already been poisoned.

For Christians all around the world, it feels like Groundhog Day. We wake up to new scandals every day. There are many ways a church can hurt a person, as we saw in the previous chapter. This kind of betrayal is uniquely suited to creating a mid-faith crisis because it turns saints into cynics almost instantly. When you've followed a shepherd for decades, what happens when you realize he led you astray? How do we find authentic faith when our leaders and mentors turn out to be con artists? It's no wonder so many of us are left with a Christianity that once looked shiny and inspiring and now seems rotten to the core. *This* Christianity *is* rotten to the core. Do a little digging and we find a long, long trail of ego-driven wolves cosplaying as shepherds all the way back to . . . well, as far back as we can see. It's so different from the Jesus path we thought we started down. We wonder: Is the authentic way of love even real? Was it all just sleight of hand?

And what about the people and institutions that were supposed to hold these leaders accountable? All too often, when questions arose and red flags were raised, governing bodies such as boards and denominational leadership looked the other way. It wasn't merely abusive priests who drove congregants from Catholic schools and parishes, for example, but the bishops and dioceses who knew and did nothing—or at least, not nearly enough. Thus, the coverups of these scandals are often worse than the heinous crimes themselves, for they allow the harm to continue, to multiply. Perhaps these overseers believed the good outweighed the bad, or that the abusive person was too powerful to confront. Likely they believed that removing the harmful leader or even calling him out would do irreparable damage to the ministry, the mission, the kingdom of God. Whatever their motive, trust becomes broken not only with one person or one church but with the entire denomination or ministry, often with even the concept of church and faith.

The pattern has grown so predictable that even those not yet harmed start to ask: Why does this keep happening? What do we need to do to make it stop?

Let us affirm and welcome these questions, the sick feeling in our stomachs. It is right and good to feel disgust with any human who acts this way, much less the church and those we trusted to point us to Jesus, to the God of love and redemption. It is right to get angry with leaders like Ravi and the ministry that enabled his widespread abuse. It's right and good to question whether this pattern is a feature or a bug of the American church.

But the haunting questions turn inward too. I (Jason) ask myself: Why was I so surprised to hear the truth of my distant mentor? He was big, and he fell hard. Did I think my celebrity would be immune from the cultural adage just because he was a Christian celebrity? And most importantly, What sort of person have I been trying to become all this time?

Maybe we thought we could use these powers for good. Wouldn't full stadiums bring people to Jesus and glory to God? Wouldn't YouTube sermons with a million views showcase the beauty of the gospel of Jesus Christ? Wouldn't a growing Instagram or TikTok following make Jesus' beauty seem compelling to a thirsty world?

Clearly, it hasn't worked out that way. Men and women are leaving the church in unprecedented numbers, naming the hypocrisy and abuse of their leaders as the reason why.

Let us acknowledge our propensity to worship. This is how we're wired. When we build stages, we cannot resist seeing the person standing upon it as powerful, worthy, a god. One celebrity church went so far as to cordon off a VIP section in their stadium seating for visiting superstars.[4]

Nothing about this behavior is native to our faith in the God-made-flesh Jesus who lacked a place to lay his head, who walked among the working poor in Roman-occupied Judea.

Rather, they are appropriations of American consumerism. This isn't Christianity; it's just Western worship.

BETRAYAL

If you paid thousands of dollars for a guide to lead you to all the most compelling and transcendent historical sites throughout Europe but the guide stole your money and left you in a cheap hotel in Branson, Missouri, you would be devastated. The hopes and dreams you worked toward for years, as you saved money and planned itineraries, are all left broken, with nothing but disappointment and ill-treatment to show for it.

For thousands of us, this is our mid-faith crisis. The men and women we trusted to lead us to Jesus turned out to be heading entirely in the opposite direction. We've been taken, conned. Our guides did not merely fail here and there, as all humans will, but egregiously worshiped an entirely different Lord and Savior: power, money, sex, themselves. We're left with years of our lives (and sometimes hard-earned money too) down the drain, our hopes dashed, our trust gutted.

This feeling is *betrayal*. It's important that we name this. That we sit with it. We trusted our leaders and heroes with all the hope and earnestness the good news of Jesus inspired in us, and we were betrayed.

Our heroes don't only betray us; they also disciple us down a path that does not lead to life, does not lead to Jesus and a healthy expression of faith. Early on we envision for ourselves a future of doing great things for God, of becoming a person of influence. We end up part of the same system that hurt us so badly, that derailed our own faith journey. We hurt those coming behind us in turn. We hurt ourselves when it all falls apart. It's no wonder we're left feeling lost and devastated.

When our heroes of the faith show their true colors, when we realize they were serving their own appetites for power, wealth, influence, or sex and *not* teaching us how to follow Jesus, love God, and love each other through the fruits of the Spirit, we find ourselves with little but a broken heart to show for our investment, utterly disoriented and lost.

In our hypothetical travel scenario, we would report the tour guide and his company. We wouldn't give up on Europe or believe for a second that this musty hotel in rural America was the best Vienna, Paris, and Venice had to offer. Similarly, the problem was never Jesus. Jesus—the God who humbles himself, who meets us in our weakness and is close to the brokenhearted, who pours out rather than grasps, who suffers for his enemies rather than make them suffer, who insists the most important commandment is that we love each other—is still here, waiting with open hands.

How can we learn to find this God, know this God, and serve this God, when we've been so turned around by untrustworthy guides? Maybe we're like Israel, crying out for a king to save us, to define us (1 Samuel 8:4-5). If we're honest, maybe we didn't want to follow the dusty footprints of Christ down a path of service and compassion. Jesus did say that following him required dying to ourselves, picking up a cross, turning our backs on the comforts of success. It makes sense that instead we wanted a champion.

"Don't do it," the prophet Samuel warned us. He knew how heroes turn on their followers. Kings steal sons for war and daughters for sex. They build palaces they don't need with muscles they don't own. They turn their sycophants to slaves (1 Samuel 8:10-14).

The psalmist echoed the warning many years later: "Some may trust in chariots and some in horses, / but we trust in the name of the LORD our God" (Psalm 20:7). We dismissed this also.

Then Jesus came, "in very nature God" yet not considering this status something to be grasped, something to hold on to (Philippians 2:5-8). Instead, Jesus made himself nothing, a servant, eschewing riches and slipping away from crowds. God laid down his life, for us. *For us.* He came not as a prince of the Roman Empire or even a citizen but as a not entirely legitimate baby in a peasant family of an occupied nation. He hung out with the working poor, the diseased, the ones with few earthly options. He healed people in shadows, hid from the paparazzi, and railed against "the deceitfulness of wealth" (Mark 4:19). He never wrote a book or left anything behind but the symbols of his own broken body and blood. He ate with "sinners" in their homes while angrily confronting the "good" religious leaders for doing so much damage to the people under their influence.

A few decades later, his brother James summed up Jesus' ethic this way:

My brothers and sisters, believers in our glorious Lord Jesus Christ must not show favoritism. Suppose a man comes into your meeting wearing a gold ring and fine clothes, and a poor man in filthy old clothes also comes in. If you show special attention to the man wearing fine clothes and say, "Here's a good seat for you," but say to the poor man, "You stand there" or "Sit on the floor by my feet," have you not discriminated among yourselves and become judges with evil thoughts? (James 2:1-4)

WHERE WE GO FROM HERE

How do we start over when the giants we followed have fallen, when we realize they were not looking to or walking toward Jesus? When we realize we were following a wolf not a shepherd, a cult leader not a servant?

The thing is, we do learn how to live by watching others who have gone before us, attempting to fit our feet into their prints. The question is, What sort of people are we watching? There's a difference between following predators gaining fame by exploiting trusting fans and following fellow humans who are actively, yet imperfectly submitting their lives to God.

I (Catherine) know a woman named Rachel, who, well into her eighties, spent whatever energy she had volunteering behind the scenes to make sure her community's after-school program for at-risk kids stayed in the black and could pay its bills. A retired accountant, she quietly balanced the books each evening. Few people knew she was doing it, much less how pivotal she was to the success of these kids, many of whom have now graduated from college, the first in their families, now giving back to the community in a hundred ways.

My large, suburban church has many pastors, but the one who looks like Jesus to me is almost never on the stage. When Pastor Joe sees me—or anyone, however low in status—he's never too busy to go out of his way to shake our hands and ask how we're doing with genuine interest and warmth. I've seen Joe with his arms full of refugee children as he talks their parents through logistic problems with a patient, encouraging, compassionate tone. I've seen him pinned to a metal folding chair for hours, when one of these kids fell asleep on his lap. I suspect many of my fellow church members don't know this man's name, face, or title—but my husband and I point him out to our kids because he looks like Jesus to us.

One more: an older couple, John and Susan, who are nondescript in every way. They don't turn any heads, don't have an online presence; their names will be forgotten by all but a few shortly after they die. But for as long as I've known them—for decades—they have been quietly chipping away at other people's educational debt, paying off other people's medical bills, paving the way for young parents to buy diapers or young professionals to buy a car without debt. I'm confident that 90 percent of the people who know these two have no idea what they do. They have no wealth to speak of, but they tirelessly use what they have to make the path easier for those with less.

None of these people call attention to themselves. Each of them would be shocked to discover that I've noticed. But Rachel, Pastor Joe, John, and Susan show me the path toward Jesus, toward a faith that is Christlike. Each would be genuinely baffled and embarrassed to discover I considered each of them a hero. Should we worship them? No. Should we assume that beneath all this they don't have broken, messy, sinful patterns of their own? No. Of course they do. But they are disciples.

INVISIBLE HEROES

This kind of noticing can be a first step toward rewiring our brains—or as Paul might say, "the renewing of your mind" (Romans 12:2). What we called good and godly for so long we now recognize as broken, if not evil. There is no sense in trying to defend it, and there is great risk in hitching our expectations to a new spiritual rockstar. People on stages—or writing books—might have some helpful things to say, but they make lousy gods. Instead of looking for heroes, maybe it's time to look around us for those who are truly worthy of praise.

Let's begin with a list, a list of godly characteristics. Not the ones many of us learned first: bold, brash, commanding (maybe harsh), confident (maybe arrogant). Instead, picture Jesus on the dusty ground, washing his disciples' feet—to their utter disgust, as even a slave could refuse such a distasteful task (John 13:1-17). Embarrassing. Yet Jesus pushed back on their critique, saying that this is the way it must be with all Jesus-followers. Not status seeking, but service. Not service that leads to applause but service that leads to a more compassionate, gracious life for everyone.

And just a few hours later, God surrendered his life, choosing to die for his enemies rather than fight them, rather than take a path of less subversive love.

What else goes on this new list? We pray you will explore that question through quiet reading and meditation, and discussion with other people in mid-faith crisis. Not just for a moment but over the course of days and weeks and months, we pray that your eyes will open to find beautiful and compelling sights of Jesus right here in the messiness of your real life, and you will know it when you see it. But here are a few words to get us started:

- Humility
- Love
- Compassion
- Service
- Gentleness
- Faithfulness
- Generosity

Now, make a second list. On this list, place the names of new heroes of the faith whose shoes you might consider placing your feet into, whose footprints might actually lead you toward Jesus. This will be harder because they will not have spent a lifetime ensuring you know their names. They don't get massive likes on Instagram or followers on TikTok. They probably don't have a podcast, and their church services do not broadcast on cable. Instead, they're the ones letting themselves into the church offices after hours, using volunteer time to make sure the children's ministry has what it needs to keep feeding hungry kids and serving exhausted parents. They're the ones who serve on thankless committees, or perhaps don't have time for committees because they are at home loving needy family members and neighbors, unseen and unheeded. They slip cash into a card (unsigned) when a family can't meet their medical bills. They stop by to visit those cut off from community: the elderly in their homes, the sick in the hospital and nursing homes, the prisoners behind bars, the immigrants at the border.

These heroes are all but invisible. But these giants walk among us, friends. They do, if we can learn to see them, to value them. They aren't cool or popular or flashy. They are faithful.

This is our mission, if we choose to accept it. We've been left betrayed and broken by those who promised to lead us to Jesus—and maybe to a stage of influence of our own. If we're honest, we may have left a wake of disillusioned followers behind us too. Now, disoriented, brokenhearted, and beaten down, we have a choice. Do we give up on Jesus altogether? Do we follow the path of power, hoping to make a name for ourselves even so? Or do we go back to the beginning, starting over, relearning what it means to lead, to follow, and to begin a new discipleship path to the true kingdom?

The good news is, if we learn to see these all-but-invisible heroes of the kingdom, not only might we find Jesus in our midst, but we might actually do some quiet good ourselves. We might become the heroes we were looking for, after all.

PRACTICE

Finding New Heroes

If you learned the rhythms of faith by watching or learning from celebrities, it's likely that you too are looking for the path that leads to Jesus rather than wealth and power. If your mid-faith crisis was sparked by unworthy heroes, we invite you to reconsider what a life of faith looks like as demonstrated by those on the margins of society rather than on the platform of influence. Using a journal, sketchpad, voice note app, or anything that appeals to you, explore the lists described above in more depth.

- What kinds of people did you look to as religious icons or mentors before? What attracted you to them? What made them feel godly to you?
- Write out the list of quiet, hidden characteristics of Jesus-followers, as described above. What do you want to be searching for going forward?
- Now, think through what people you know who quietly and humbly exemplify those qualities. How could you invest in these people and their daily work for God's kingdom? What could you do to spend time with them and learn from them? What could you do to support them?
- Now, think of the people who are carefully fitting their feet into your own footprints. What words would they use to describe you? What would you like to be known for? Do these aspects fit the Christlike descriptions you wrote out earlier? What needs to change? What tangible steps can you begin with this week?
- Share some of this with a close friend or group of friends. Invite them to do a similar exercise and consider who you worship and why.

Something to Listen To

- "Tightrope," Jon Guerra
- "All the Poor and Powerless," All Sons & Daughters

|||||||||||||||||||||||||||||||||||||||||||||||||||||||||||||||||||||||||||| ***Something to Read***

- *Our Church Speaks: An Illustrated Devotional of Saints from Every Era and Place,* Ben Lansing and D. J. Marotta
- *The Way of the Dragon or the Way of the Lamb: Searching for Jesus' Path of Power in a Church That Has Abandoned It,* Jamin Goggin and Kyle Strobel
- *Might from the Margins: The Gospel's Power to Turn the Tables on Injustice,* Dennis R. Edwards

|||||||||||||||||||||||||||||||||||||||||||||||||||||||||||||||||||||||||||||||||||||||||||||||||||||||||||||

6

WHEN OUR PRAYERS FELL SILENT

Of all the faith garments worn threadbare from hard use, prayer may be the most tattered and frayed. Childhood bedtime wishes morphed into teenage pleadings and in adulthood have become an uphill climb. Along the way we've walked a million miles, collected a thousand memories and a hundred callouses. We're tired. What should be—and hopefully still will be—a comfortable and comforting habit feels harder than ever by now.

Because prayer is a practice many of us learn as soon as we can speak and continue to pursue throughout life, perhaps our progression through the stages of faith is easier to see here than in other aspects of life. We know we pray differently now than we did as little children, or as energetic young converts. The types of prayer we gravitate to—and what we hope to accomplish through prayer—change as the years go by.

Do we still believe in prayer? Yes, but it's complicated. Do we believe God is with us and hears the cries of our hearts? We do, at least most of the time. Do we believe God cares? Oh, we hope so. Do we think God shifts the course of the universe in response to a billion utterances several times each minute? That's hard to imagine. Have we experienced rare, precious moments of God's presence through prayer when *something* seems to happen? Yes. Yes, we have.

But these prayer-walking boots are worn out, and our feet are sore.

HOW PRAYER STARTED

How did you learn to pray, way back when? Many of us who first encountered God in the Inherited Faith stage of childhood were introduced to prayer as a time to talk to God. And we talked a lot. The Bible tells us to bring all our prayers and petitions before God, knowing that God will meet our needs—so we did. Before dinner, before bed, during Sunday school, we babbled on about our sick pets, our bumps and bruises, every vulnerable joy and sorrow in our young hearts. Back then, God was something between a distant parent and Santa Claus—not really available but likely to provide what we needed if we told him about it.

I (Catherine) was turning ten years old the first time I reconsidered this approach. Too excited to sleep the previous night, relishing my last hours in the single digits, my brain was spinning and summoned a long-buried memory. I jumped up wide awake, afraid for my life.

Years before, I had hatched a genius plan: choose a particular age, the definition of a long and fulfilling life, then earnestly pray God would allow me to die on the birthday of that year (after presents and cake, of course). This would take away all the guesswork and worry about unknowns like accidents, illness, and death. Why not lock in your future early on?

The ripe old age I chose was ten. Of course, I had no context or life experience to inform this bold decision. And now, with just hours left to go on this earth, I leapt from bed and ran to find my parents.

Amazingly, they were unconcerned.

Yet my prayers had been earnest and consistent. I had prayed in faith, fully believing with all my heart that God would hear and grant my request. Like the righteous believer in James (a book I memorized word for word in fourth grade), I had asked without wavering or doubting. Surely my prayers would be "powerful and effective" (James 5:16).

Plus, while I prayed these childish prayers for death, I had also been praying for a brother or sister. Even after my parents sat by my bed and gently told me I could stop asking God (their doctors were sure no little baby would join our family—now or ever), I was determined. I would pray without ceasing, no matter what they said.

And sure enough, a few months later my parents were back with news: my mom was pregnant. I would have a baby brother. That sealed the deal for me. Nine-going-on-ten-year-old Catherine viewed prayer as a wish list to offer God—a to-do list, even. And therefore, my life was in grave danger.

But my tenth birthday came and went—cake, party, presents, lasagna dinner, all of it. No one died.

As I grew older and looked back on that night, my takeaway was gratitude that God knows better than we do. A loving parent will say no to many pleading requests for bright-colored cleaning chemicals and sharp, shiny tools, no matter how badly their beloved toddlers want them. Who am I to know what I really need, compared to God's infinite knowledge and care? Rather than shake my faith, this vivid experience became for me a doorway into Confident Faith, into a carefully thought-through trust in God's work in our lives.

But since that day when my faith was strengthened by God's failure to answer, there's been so much water under the bridge. I've been abandoned and deeply harmed by people who were supposed to love and protect me. Felt all hope for goodness shatter around me. Sat in the room while my best friends' baby died in their arms. Bristled with anger when a friend chirped, "Praise God!" upon finding a good parking spot while nearly ninety million displaced people in our world can't find a home country. Carried stories—my own and others'—almost too terrible to believe.

Yet, I've also seen long-unsolved ailments disappear from my body during prayer. Felt God draw so near to me it changed my life's direction. Experienced spiritual and emotional healing from wounds I didn't even know I had. Been prompted to do things so clearly God's voice was almost audible. Seen those in desperate need provided for in nearly supernatural ways.

Thus far into my journey, it's not God or even prayer I doubt so much as our confidence in prayer, the hubris of our own causation, and our own willingness to overlook profound suffering in the world. When a friend's flight delivers her to vacation safe and sound, she posts to Facebook that "God knew how much I needed restful time away." But another friend texts me that, due to cancellations from the same airport on the same day, she missed getting to her sister's deathbed in time to say goodbye. Well, if God is to be praised in the first instance, is he to be blamed in the second?

What are we supposed to make of a prayer-theology so confident in God's will and our prayer-to-result causation, and so unaware of our own privilege and dumb luck? Do we really think God is granting some of us luxury items simply because we asked—and does this mean that victims of genocide and sexual assault just didn't have enough prayer coverage for God to act on their behalf?

You can see how my brain starts spinning into faith crisis. The same compassion and conviction that once prompted me to pray now prompts me to question almost everything.

If God is good and loving, doesn't God already care? Does God only act in response to a popularity contest or poll? And if God *isn't* good and loving, if God *does* need convincing to do the right and decent thing, then what is the point of prayer at all? Dabble in prayer long enough, and many of us end up facing these kinds of questions. A banquet of rich prayer practices, passed down through a thousand generations, was watered down into a formula: hands folded, eyes closed. Wholehearted faith and passionate prayers caved in on themselves and started to crush us, leaving us with nothing but profound feelings of abandonment and confusion.

So that's how it started, and a bit of how it's going. I don't think I'm alone. The complexities of (mostly unsuccessfully) asking the divine to alter the world on our behalf is one of the most universally probed quandaries of faith. For some of us, the dream burst hard and fast, leaving trauma and debris in its place. For others, it's been a slow leak draining away over time, leaving us deflated and empty and confused. Many of us are weary now, with little faith that our words matter at all.

To find a way forward through Mid-Faith, I desperately need prayer to be something other than using our words to tell God what to do. Everything about that feels like a bad idea to me, now.

PRAYER WARRIORS

For me (Jason) prayer was always about words. In my circles, *intercessor* was viewed as a spiritual office, like pastor and teacher. Prayer became a specialized skill, a badge for the super spiritual: we were "prayer warriors." We saw the brokenness in our world, so we dropped to our knees in battle. Loved ones were fighting diseases; there were natural disasters, violence, and evil all around. Worse, people were dying without Jesus.

These were the enemies and our weapon was prayer. With our words we changed the world, impacted the physical and spiritual realms. If we woke in the night, we took it as a sign: time to pray. If we didn't rise to the task, our loved ones might suffer.

What a strange delusion of power. We treated the fate of our fellow humans as if they depended not on a loving Creator but on our midnight pleas, as though our lives were rooted not in God's care but in the performance of prayer warriors. But these were God-sized burdens, and it was too much for us to carry around. The weight of the world—war and peace, life and death, joy and suffering, even heaven and hell—was far too heavy for our mortal shoulders.

Looking back, I'm convinced we were not wasting our time. Jesus invites us to bring our petitions to God. God tells us to ask for help. But God also tells us to trust. To be still. To be thankful. To rest. To meditate. To contemplate. To dwell. To bring God our groanings too deep for words.

I loved words then, and I still do. I love the ways you can shape them to build stories, to leave impressions, to make people cry. A teacher once told me that language was God's greatest gift to us because language was the foundation of relationships. Without language, how can you know a person? That idea stuck with me. Maybe that's why Jack's diagnosis hit me as hard as it did.

Jack is my third child, my oldest son. He hit most of his developmental markers until he was two, but then something changed. His vocabulary disappeared. He stopped making eye contact. He began wandering around the house ignoring us, flapping spatulas in front of his face. We figured out what it was before the diagnosis came, but seeing the word on paper hit me hard: autism. It soon became clear that his was the kind of autism in which words would be rare.

Of course, this led me to prayer. Jack would grow up in a world that didn't understand him, and he would deal with a host of comorbid conditions that would increase the difficulty of his life: obsessive compulsive disorder, seizures, and raging anxiety. So I prayed a lot. Which is to say, I used all my words when I came to God.

"Lord, help us to understand why he is screaming!"

"God, don't let him run out onto the road again!"

"Please, please, please, let him sleep!"

But the thing we prayed for most was the gift of language. How could we know our son if we couldn't converse with him? Isn't language the foundation of relationship?

It didn't occur to me then what an odd bargain I was trying to strike, using words to beg for words. And that's the problem with viewing prayer primarily—or exclusively—as convincing God to act. Prayer can become all about how persuasive we can be at getting God to do what we want.

God didn't answer my prayers anyway. By the time I reached forty, Jack was a teenager, still functionally nonverbal, still wrestling with the same comorbid conditions he'd always had.

So what happened to all those prayers I prayed in my twenties and thirties? What happened to yours, the ones that didn't get approved through the bureaucracy of heaven? Did they ever receive a hearing? Did they accidentally get deleted from God's hard drive? Or did God simply say no?

Church history has been far from silent on the issue of prayer. Believers throughout the centuries have wrestled with these exact questions, and proposed profound answers. I wasn't entirely blind to the answers they offered, but neither was I all that interested in ideas outside my immediate theological grid. In my charismatic circles, we were usually looking for mechanical help. *How* do I get God to answer? *How* do I pray with authority? *How* can I change my heart such that God will hear me? If the prayers of the righteous "availeth much" (James 5:16 KJV), how do I become more righteous? I didn't want wisdom. I wanted results.

And that's fair. When our hearts are aching, we don't want to talk theology. In a crisis, we're not drawn to learn from monks and sages; we don't have time to ponder theories. We just need things to work. We just want the pain to go away.

We can't deny our experiences with unanswered prayer. Not when our pending requests have piled up like junk-mail advertisements. That's the thing that sucks the vitality out of prayer for many of us. It's not that we don't believe anymore; it's just that our words feel so empty, like expired coupons that were never a good deal to begin with.

Once that pile of unanswered prayer gets high enough, you realize prayer can't be about using your words to make God do your bidding. There's a time to clench your fists and yell at the sky, but there's a time to open your palms and surrender. A time to beg God for daily bread, a time to breathe, "Your will be done."

UNHEALED

A few years ago, I (Catherine) suffered a traumatic brain injury that turned out to be far worse than I realized at the time. What my doctors pronounced would take weeks to heal stretched into months, then years. At first, friends were eager to pray for me, asking to place their hands on my head and in faith ask God for my healing. I was grateful for their care, and grateful for their prayers. I craved it, actually, nearly crying with relief each time someone offered. I felt so isolated in those months, so desperate for a friend to cut a hole in the roof and lower me down to Jesus.[1]

But the moment my praying friends opened their eyes I saw them look expectantly at me: Did it work? Had they done it? Was I healed?

Did it work? I was not healed, that part was easy to answer. I believe God can heal, and I think it's good to ask for healing—but I didn't see it that day. My pain and long-term damage did not lift even one iota during or after these heartfelt petitions. I could not produce the evidence my friends so badly hoped to see—and the burden of being asked for it so often added to my burden.

But I would not say those prayers didn't work. They bonded me to my community when I needed companionship—at least, to whatever degree people stuck by me when I had no fruit of healing to offer them. Prayer allowed me to feel cared for, not entirely alone in my darkness and fears. And prayer bonded me to God when I was desperate for him. Prayer became a path toward the green pastures and quiet waters I longed for yet could not find on my own. When my friends lifted their hands and voices on my behalf, I felt enveloped by a love that transcended my terrifying circumstances.

As I spent hour upon hour alone in the dark so my brain could heal, as it became abundantly clear God was not using prayer to magically fix things, these worship lyrics lingered in my addled brain day after long day: "I'm no longer a slave to fear; I am a child of God."[2] I could almost hear God's voice saying, "This season of suffering isn't what you need liberation from—this season of suffering *is* the liberation."

Friend, I have no idea what this means. I didn't understand it then, and I don't understand it now. But while prayer did not make me healthy (years later, I'm still not fully recovered), prayer did get me through.

Recently I found these words in my journal, from my early days of parenthood:

> Asher is becoming quite the communicative little fellow. His coos and babbles and giggles are heart-melting, and I am spellbound, absolutely unable to do anything other than participate in this conversation.
>
> My dad overheard one of these tête-à-têtes recently and mentioned that, after long months of hard baby-raising work and sacrifice, the road is beginning to go both ways; this little person is learning to interact with me. It doesn't really matter that his words are mean-ingless or that he doesn't know my language. What needs to be communicated is getting through clearly: we enjoy each other. And he looks to me to care for him—in times of comfort and times of discomfort.
>
> Maybe this is the best way to understand prayer. None of us know enough to really comprehend prayer: our most eloquent, theologically, purely motivated prayers aren't much more than babbling to an infinite Creator. But God cares for us, loves us, stays close to us, even when we can't or won't pursue a relationship with him— so how much sweeter when we do, even if halting, unbalanced, confused, and self-centeredly?

This is where I find comfort, when I ascribe so little power or causation to my words: if God is this close, holding us in his arms or sitting with us on the floor as we throw our tantrums, then we don't need to craft a message or send a telegraph. We just need to lift our eyes, open our hands, and lean against his arms. The fact is, we really are children in the grand scheme of things.

OUT OF WORDS

Over the years, Jack found ways to circumvent his lack of language. In lieu of words, he used gestures, movie quotes, a bit of sign language, and a bit of texting.

It was never predictable. His efforts came and went, and we learned not to put too much hope in any medium of communication. At seventeen years old, he wasn't using any language with regularity.

Still, we found ways to connect. One afternoon, I (Jason) took him to a restaurant called Buffalo Wild Wings. He didn't tell me what he wanted to eat or drink, but he didn't need to. I'm his dad. I know he's too young for an IPA, and he won't eat chicken wings, but boy does he love french fries and lemon-lime soda. So that's what I ordered. I didn't fill our time with words, which can be so frustrating for him. Why would I spoil it? He had his music, his big blue headphones, and his favorite laminated picture that he carries around with him everywhere. More than that, he had his dad.

For the next hour, we sat together sharing fries in relative silence. To an outsider, it probably looked like we were ignoring one another. But that's so far from the truth. We were sharing a quiet moment. We were together.

This is how I'm learning to embrace prayer now. Like Jack, I run out of words, and sometimes find them frustrating. What do you say when your heart is broken? How many different ways can I describe the same pain, the same worries, the same unmet requests? Is that even what God wants from our time together, for me to fill every moment with the sound of my own voice? Is that even what I want?

No. I have come to believe my old teacher was wrong about the foundation of relationships. Language is one of God's greatest gifts, to be sure. But there's something else that comes first: presence. Presence comes before language. That's true with our own children, and it's true with God. Presence is the foundation of our relationship and the true essence of prayer.

And yes, we ask for God's help and intervention—sometimes humbly, sometimes in desperate grief, sometimes with burning rage. Being open and vulnerable with God about our fears, needs, hopes, and feelings—excited or brokenhearted or anything in between—is very different from telling God what to do. I think of Job, who talked to God incessantly. Even in suffering he talked and talked and talked to God. But it wasn't until Job ran out of words and fell silent in God's presence that he began to feel relief.

Of course, some people come at prayer from a different angle. Maybe you've always felt comfortable resting in God's presence but need encouragement to consider voicing your thoughts and requests. Many faith traditions don't encourage spontaneous wordy prayers, so the idea of dialoguing with God can be shocking! This is why we need each other. There's something freeing in realizing that we are dust, vapor, as short-lived as the flowers of the field. We will not find peace or goodness in carrying the world's burdens, in dictating instructions to God, yet we are invited to bring our full selves, inviting us to draw near to his presence. God knows what our hearts are burning for, grieving over. And I'm convinced God truly wants to be with us, even when we're screaming in pain, even when we're kicking and punching, even when there's nothing left to say. God delights in us, holds us close like Catherine did her son Asher. We don't need to boss God around or give orders. We don't need to beg or plead. But we're invited to trust, to rest, to pour out our hearts and draw near.

We're the kids after all.

DAILY BREAD

So, with our prayer boots so worn out, our feet so calloused and torn, and so far to go in this journey, how do we wield the power of prayer to get what we want and need out of life, out of God? Maybe we don't—and that's a hard pill to swallow.

It feels weird to say this but here goes: God is worth knowing even though he doesn't obey my instructions. It's worth spending time with God, worth practicing how to live in God's presence, even though we can't control what God does, even though we know God won't make all our dreams come true or remove all our pain.

Before we're ready to learn a new way to be with God, we may need to grieve the death of what we thought prayer was, what we hoped and believed prayer was. We may even need to grieve the death of who or what we thought God was and would do for us in exchange for seeking him. There's profound disappointment there, and disillusionment too. We aren't the

world changers we thought we would be. God—and prayer—
and life—aren't nearly as straightforward as we assumed.

Saint Teresa of Avila described prayer as "nothing else than
a close sharing between friends; it means taking time fre-
quently to be alone with him who we know loves us."[3] Not a
way for us mortals to control the universe or change the world;
not a way for us to rid our lives of all we fear and replace it with
all we long for. Instead, prayer is a way of imbibing courage
and strength to continue this long, hard journey of life by
being with someone who knows and loves us perfectly from
beginning to end.

So where do we go from here? If our childhood dreams
have been crushed, if the journey of prayer all these years has
exhausted and disoriented us, how can prayer be a spiritual
discipline that leads us back to life—not just to more disappointment and death?

Jesus taught his friends how to pray using what we now call
the Lord's Prayer—and it's a good place to start:

Jesus told them, "When you pray, say:
'Father, uphold the holiness of your name. Bring in
your kingdom. Give us the bread we need for today.
Forgive us our sins, for we also forgive everyone who
has wronged us. And don't lead us into temptation.'"
(Luke 11:2-4 CEB)

There's much here that might help: ask God to help us get
through each day, remember to keep God's kingdom central,
help us forgive and be forgiven, reach out for strength to stay
on track. Meditate on God's character. Give thanks for life's

gifts—both simple and profound. Learn to slow down and be silent, relearning how to find wisdom and beauty in each day, in each breath.

Daily bread, daily bread, daily bread.

As we lean away from prayer as words, words, words, we're both grateful to realize that *prayer* is an awkwardly broad term for at least a dozen spiritual practices, each with a rich history. The one word *prayer* represents practices of praise, thanksgiving, intercession, and more; we may read from a liturgy, sing a song, repeat a word or phrase, speak our minds, or simply remain silent. To mix things up, we can walk a prayer labyrinth, light a candle, or kneel in a prayer chapel; we might read a psalm, open a prayer book. We might pray the Prayer of Examen,[4] the Jesus Prayer,[5] the Lord's Prayer, or countless more.

Perhaps our problem isn't that we made prayer too big but too small—that we turned the focus on ourselves and missed the bigger picture. Telling God what we want or need isn't the same as confessing sin or giving thanks, each of which is different from the quiet contemplativeness of breath prayers during a walk through the forest. And yes, some of them may make us recoil from past spiritual missteps, but others sound like an invitation to life.

Maybe Jesus' prayers in the garden and Jesus' prayers on the cross are the examples we need in this mid-faith season of suffering and doubt. Jesus begged for his suffering to ease— begged so hard and long that his anguish looked and felt like bleeding, like dying. But his suffering did not ease, not in the slightest—nor would it in this life. Later that night he prayed again, this time asking for help to surrender: "If it is not possible for this cup to be taken away unless I drink it, may your will be done" (Matthew 26:42).

Just a few hours later, Jesus' final words were these: "Father, into your hands I commit my spirit" (Luke 23:46).

Friends, some days that might be as far as you can go. But if that prayer was enough for Jesus at his darkest hours, it's good enough for us in ours: God, here I am. So tired, so worn out. Far too exhausted to hold on to hope, with all this pain and sorrow still here. I put myself into your hands.

That's a prayer we can honestly repeat every day.

PRACTICE

|||||||||||||||||||||||||||||||||||||||||||||||||||||||||||||||||||||||||||||||||| *Prayer as Presence*

If your faith journey began with an expectation that you could (and must) attempt to control or sway God, you too may be feeling exhausted by now, and let down. If you were primarily taught to approach God with words or if you were never taught how to bring your own heart and words to God, we invite you to consider a spiritual practice of spending unpressured time with God.

Find a quiet place and a comfortable chair to sit in. Take a full minute to be silent in God's presence. A minute is short, but it might feel far too long, too awkward. That's okay. Just stay there for a moment. Open your hands and face your palms upward.

As thoughts and concerns come to mind—and they will—briefly turn them over to God: "Lord, I bring my daughter to you once again. I ask you to heal her, to make her whole, and to bring her back to us."

Then, release that prayer to God. Turn your palms upside down as if you are placing that loved one or situation into his hands. As you do so, say, "Your will be done."

Then, return to rest quietly in God's presence. Resist the urge to end quickly, or to fill the space with more explanation. Remember, God already knows your pains and your fears. So let him sit next to you. Just be together in the silence. As more urgent thoughts come to mind, move them over to God's hands and return to the quiet place.

If you are someone who has never felt empowered to bring your words and heart to God, be bold! God is eager to meet with you. If you are someone who only knows how to approach God with words, be still! God is with you in the silence as well.

Rest there. Enjoy the presence of the one who knows your needs and delights in you.

Fill the silence with delight. What sounds do you hear? What sights do you see? If any of them are calming or lovely, enjoy them with God. Thank God for them briefly, then return to the place of quiet.

Once you get the hang of quieting yourself in God's presence, you can take it on the road. Wherever you enjoy being, God is already there. Try this companionable silence in the forest, at the beach, or even in the car, at your desk, or in the checkout line at the grocery store.

Something to Listen To

- "The Silence of God," Andrew Peterson
- "Last Words," Jon Foreman

||||||||||||||||||||||||||||||||||||||||||||||||||||||||||||||||||||||| ***Something to Read***

- *Prayer: Finding the Heart's True Home*, Richard J. Foster
- *How to Pray: A Simple Guide for Normal People*, Pete Greig
- *Help, Thanks, Wow*, Anne Lamott

|||||||||||||||||||||||||||||||||||||||||||||||||||||||||||||||||||||||||||||||||||||||||||||||||||||||||||||||||||||||||||||||||||

7

WHEN SUFFERING CONSUMED US

My (Catherine's) family was hiking through the dense woods of one of America's national parks when we stumbled upon a long-abandoned church. When I say "long," I mean services have not been held here in probably two hundred years. Generations of trees and foliage enveloped this small building, the log and lumber walls crumbling to show us the one-room sanctuary inside. We detoured from the path out of my love for forgotten history, the tell-tale signs of life lived long before my own.

But as we waded through the deep grasses and scrambled over boulders trying to get back to our hiking path, I discovered something even more astonishing: the abandoned church's cemetery. Now I was spellbound. I picked my way down row after row, taking in what information I could: a small, crooked stone emerging from the undergrowth here or there, engravings nearly worn away by time. It was like stumbling upon a forgotten time capsule, but one row stood out to me.

Twelve tiny stones, one after the next, each engraved with two dates just days, weeks, or months apart: a trail of beloved children who died in their infancy or at least in early childhood. At the end of this devastating queue was a slightly larger stone with a name I couldn't make out, then the words "Beloved Wife and Mother." There were decades between her birth date and death, but not much more than two. Not as many as three. Then, finally, after her, stood one stone more: her husband, their father, a man who lived into middle age. From the evidence of this long-abandoned gravesite, he was neither remarried nor survived by living children when he died.

I stood there, lost in the lives of these real, historic girls and boys, this woman, this man. What must it have been like to marry young, for pregnancy to follow soon after, to hold their newborn in their arms—only to have her die days later? But this story played out not one or even two or three times but twelve, each year bringing a new pregnancy and childbirth, with all the work and hope and sacrifice that go with them— only to end in fresh tragedy, fresh loss. In fact, her short life held very little but this repeating cycle until, in the final blow, childbirth took both mother and baby, leaving behind a man to live out his grief alone.

This long-ago family stayed with me as we hiked home in the setting sun. Their short lives were saturated with suffering, so full of grief there could hardly have been room for much else. This was all they got. All that's left now are these most basic details, nearly buried in the forest, slowly worn away by the sun and rain.

What stayed with me most is how different their lives were from anything we are taught to expect—and yet, how relatively common their experience has been throughout human history.

Today we hope for long lives, have reason to believe we will not die in childbirth, that our babies will not be struck down one by one. We expect that, for the most part, we will pursue happiness and fulfillment with sadness and suffering relegated to the margins, with an occasional interruption to survive before we get back to the main story.

But for many, many people the opposite has been true. Most people in history lost children, giving birth to many, desperately hoping a few would survive. Millions experience war, abuse, oppression, poverty, tragedy. For many, many, life is suffering—with occasional interruptions of joy that fade all too quickly before returning to the main story of anguish.

In our modern life, and modern faith, we aren't necessarily taught to expect this or trained to prepare for it. For many of us, the How It Started of our faith is a carefree belief in a God who promises to keep us safe, who has plans for us to prosper and does not wish to harm us, who declares that he will make our paths straight if we trust in him. Some of us had that story blown to pieces early on; others of us managed to stay in the bubble into our teenage years, sometimes even into adulthood. As long as we didn't suffer too much, we could believe the story that happiness was the main course and pain the aberration; we could keep the problem of suffering as an academic thought experiment. Sure, we saw awful, awful things in the news or on the prayer chain but secretly believed there had to be a reason behind why it happened to that person, that country, those people. Even if the carnage didn't make sense now, we knew it would, someday.

In the meantime, we prayed for a hedge of protection.

JANAE

Janae McWilliams was the most Texan woman I (Jason) knew, which was quite a feat seeing as she was from Central California. She spoke with an exaggerated Southern belle accent, which I'm pretty sure she faked at first but eventually became all hers. The persona fit her somehow.

I called Janae my sister, but not in the churchy, generic kind of way. Sure, she was a "sister in Christ," but she was also the person who helped me pick out anniversary presents for my wife. For sixteen years she was part of our family. We adopted her the same day our second child was born: Sara was two weeks from her due date, and we were moving into a new apartment. Just as we were loading up the furniture, her water broke. Janae sprang into action. She told us to go, assuring us that she would take charge of the moving party. We obeyed, abandoning everything to go have a baby.

When we brought our newborn into our new home, we assumed we would be met by a maze of cardboard and couch cushions, but the minute we stumbled, exhausted, onto the welcome mat, our eyes flooded with tears. The boxes were unpacked, the kitchen set up, and the beds assembled. You'd have thought we had been living there for a year. There was even a clock hanging above the kitchen table. Sara and I looked at each other in awe. Who was this woman who could love us so completely as to hang our clock?

That was when we knew she was ours. From then on, all my kids grew up with their own personal Mary Poppins (if Mary Poppins was a little more like Dolly Parton, and if she carried a massive purple purse and used words like *heinie* and *biggify*). They adored her.

Before long, we didn't dare experience life without her. She was at every birthday party and every movie night. When we moved to California, then to Oregon, she moved with us. Every time Sara got pregnant again (we had three more kids), she would tell people, "We're fixin' to have another baby!" We. We were fixin' to have that baby.

But those years weren't all sweetness. There were sicknesses and surgeries, heart defects and brain disorders. There were diagnoses. When my son Jack first regressed and lost all his vocabulary, I played it cool, telling everyone I wasn't worried. It wasn't autism. He was just a late bloomer. Janae leveled with me one day, forcing me to look her in the eye. "JasonHague" (she always ran my two names together into one), "I know you are confident that he's healthy. But if he's not, I will be here. We will go through it all together."

She was true to her word. When the diagnosis came and our world was rocked, she held onto us and wouldn't let go. Miss Janae, as the kids always called her, became Jack's biggest fan. You never saw a more devoted auntie.

But it was tragedy that sealed our bond, watching our dear friend Karen die at age thirty-three. Cancer had come for her one too many times. We were in the room when her breath ran out, when the monitor stopped beeping. Karen had been like family too. Her death was hard on all of us, but especially on Janae. It took me years to get over that night, but Janae never did.

Then, nine years after Karen's death, I contracted a vicious case of déjà vu. Janae herself got cancer.

"This is treatable," the oncologist assured us. But the feeling of inevitability sat like a stone in our stomachs.

Friends tried to comfort her in the hospital: "God's got this! You're going to be fine!" Everything in me wanted to scream, "Don't say that! You have no right to tell her that!" I believed in the power of prayer, but death had conquered Karen and was coming for each one of us eventually. I would make no assurances. Instead, I leveled with her as she had with me all those years ago, and told her, "Whatever happens, we will go through this together."

The next two months were a blur of chemo sessions and radiation doses, of frustration at the ineffectiveness of treatments, and irritation at Janae herself.

"She's got to get exercise, but she won't even take a walk," I told my wife after watching Janae ignore the oncologist's instructions. "Remember what the doctor said? This is treatable, but it's a marathon, not a sprint."

"Honey," my wife said, stopping my rant, "I don't think this is a marathon anymore."

She was right. The next day, Janae's lungs began filling with fluid, and her kidneys started to shut down. The oncologist was devastated. Everything about her prognosis had been wrong. The cancer had spread all over Janae's body. After two days in intensive care, the entire medical team pulled us into a special waiting room with Janae's mother. They told us they couldn't save her. They told us every intervention they tried caused her unbearable pain.

"I feel like we're torturing her," one of them said.

We wept with her dear mother, who had become like our mother, and conceded to the only option we had left: we moved our girl into hospice care.

That night, when she woke up on a different hospital floor suddenly free of the tangle of tubes, needles, and fussy nurses, she texted us from down the hall. It consisted of three words: "I am confused."

I still have that message on my phone, and it haunts me. Janae didn't talk like that. She used contractions. It should have said, "I'm confused," or more likely, "Im confused" without the apostrophe. Better yet, "Im mixed up," or "Can someone please tell me what the wingding is going on here?"

I took my wife's hand, and we made the long walk down the hospital hallway. Her mom was already in the room searching in vain for words of comfort. I tried to explain how her kidneys were shot, and the cancer was everywhere, but I fumbled every sentence.

"So, you're saying I'm going to die," she said in an emotionless haze.

"Yeah," I conceded.

She shook her head. "I don't know what to do with this information."

We made limp attempts to point to the silver lining. She would be with Jesus. And with Karen too! But all she could do was repeat herself. "I don't know what to do with this information."

That night, thirty of her closest friends gathered in her room and sang her favorite songs. Sara and I sat at the foot of the bed with our children, holding her hands, singing her all the way to Jesus.

She was forty-three years old.

Nothing about Janae's loss was more tragic than any other cancer story, any other early death—but it was enough to knock me off balance in a way nothing else had—not Karen's death, nor my son's heart condition, nor my other son's autism. Maybe her loss was the proverbial straw that broke the camel's back. All I know is that when she died, I didn't just feel disappointed, I felt betrayed.

Janae had given her life in service to others. How could Jesus ignore her in her own hour of need?

SURVIVING GRIEF

There's a scene in *The Chosen* where Peter and John are hurrying down the road to catch up with Jesus and the disciples.[1] They're late; their attention has been caught up in personal tragedy, and in their pain they argue as they walk. In this fictional account, Peter argues bitterly that his problem isn't faith in Jesus' ability to heal but in his grievance that Jesus chooses to heal some and not others, investing in strangers and not his own closest friends. Peter is not so sure he wants to stay close to Jesus now that he knows this. John disagrees, though not over the reality of suffering. Given how overpowering grief and trouble are in our lives, how unavoidable and pervasive, John demands to know how we can survive *except* by drawing close to Jesus, trusting in his presence to sustain and comfort us in our pain.

Though this debate is not actually recorded in the Bible, it's very believable; we encounter it in real-life conversations between Jesus-followers all the time. We know life is full of pain and trouble—at least intellectually. We know everyone dies, that everyone suffers in the meantime. But when it hits, we're blinded by pain and shock. It doesn't seem fair—whatever *fair* means. When we can no longer hold on, many of us do respond like Peter, pushing away in anger at the one Being in the universe who has all knowledge, all power, who claims to be Love and Goodness and yet seems to sit idly by as children are shot down, as cities are decimated.

Our How It Started posture around suffering seems to include a belief that our relationship with God comes with some sort of money-back guarantee—that those who suffer deserve it somehow, that pain is not random because those who put their faith in God will have a shield around them, for God plans for us to prosper and not harm us. Many of us were taught this explicitly, week after week, but nearly all of us received indirect messages and assumptions sprinkled into our songs, our rituals (or lack of rituals), the stories we told (and the stories we avoided). Believing that the good guys who really trust God can escape the worst of life's pain is a deeply embedded belief in our culture, even if we wouldn't knowingly claim to believe it. The How It's Going frame crashes in hard, for we learn far too soon that, as Job says, we are born to trouble (Job 5:7). We learn that, as Jesus promised, in this life we will have suffering (John 16:33). Even the beloved passage promising prosperity and not harm for God's people was spoken to the deeply harmed and profoundly not prospering

Babylonian exiles who heard, in the same breath as these hopeful words, the crushing blow that they would remain exiled from home and family for seventy years, a whole lifetime (Jeremiah 29:4-10).

So where is the path forward, if what we were taught to believe is nowhere in the Bible, not in line with any life lived in reality? When we realize God does not intend, did not ever promise or even suggest he would shield us from suffering, what is our next move? For many, this is the end of the road. The idea that an all-powerful, all-loving God is watching as people are kidnapped and enslaved, as generations are dehumanized and mistreated, as young boys are given the choice to be killed or learn to kill for the gangs and cartels, as women and children are violated over and over—this is just a bridge too far.

Yet for many others of us, there is a tiny spark kindled by the story that God took on flesh in order to suffer with us, to come alongside us—to allow himself to be killed rather than to kill. For us, the question is: How can we be formed such that the searing pain of the world carries us to the suffering Jesus— rather than pull us, like the tides, further and further away from the God who is close to the brokenhearted, the hope and comfort we long for? How can we, like the fictional John in *The Chosen*, find in God's presence the one reality worth betting on, the one place where meaning and comfort might be found in a world gone mad?

WHERE WE GO FROM HERE

In his sonnet "Engine Against Th'Almightie," the great English poet Malcolm Guite imagines us bringing our violent frustrations to lay siege to the divine fortress.[2] The image evokes God withdrawn behind his battlements, so we hurl our prayers toward his walls. When they fail, we let fly all the ugly accusations we have worked so hard to repress.

> We make an engine of our injuries,
> And vault at God a volley of our sorrows:
> All the despair and anger that we feel.
> The catapult of our catastrophes
> Hurls up its heavy load, and flights of arrows
> Clatter against his walls, fall back and fail.
> How can we make him feel our miseries?
> We fling back famine at him, torture, cancer,
> Is he almighty then? Has he no answer?

This scenario may feel out of bounds for the reverence we're taught God demands. Catapulting our catastrophes back at God is not how we are taught to approach the divine. Yet, this too, is part of how we have been malformed in our views of suffering, for our mothers and fathers of the faith almost always took a head-on approach with their grievances. Rather than denying or hiding them, they hurled them right back at God.

Shouting and wrestling were common for those who penned the Scriptures. These books were written by a people who were embattled and oppressed, exiled and enslaved. If anyone in history knew about suffering, it was the Hebrews. A tiny nation along a busy road, they were constantly caught up in wars they didn't want, tossed from one ancient superpower to another: Egypt to Assyria, Babylon to Persia, Greece to Syria to Rome. Even their times of independence were fraught with wars and famines and plagues—like the family with twelve headstones memorializing their babies lost in infancy—all the risk and loss that go hand in hand with living and loving. All this, the reality for God's chosen people, the ones called out to be blessed.

Where was this blessing? Where was shalom? They weren't afraid to point out the juxtaposition. Nor were they afraid to make a catapult of their catastrophes and hurl them back at God. In fact, the book of Psalms is full of such outbursts:

> Awake, Lord! Why do you sleep?
> Rouse yourself! Do not reject us forever.
> Why do you hide your face
> and forget our misery and oppression?
> We are brought down to the dust;
> our bodies cling to the ground.
> Rise up and help us. (Psalm 44:23-26)

The audacity of this poem is breathtaking. The psalmist, living through an unnamed but all-too-imaginable nightmare, practically shouts at God, accusing God of sleeping through it all. And he does not merely shout in his personal journal: these words become part of the repeated rituals of worship for the entire nation.

A few pages later, Psalm 55 goes a step further:

Listen to my prayer, O God,

do not ignore my plea. (Psalm 55:1)

There it is. These are the words, the truth of how we have felt: God has ignored us. God *is* ignoring us.

Are we really allowed to give utterance to such darkness, such rages against the Almighty? Some sixty-five psalms of lament suggest yes. Yes, it is not only okay but recommended. In fact, this brutal honesty, this screaming into the void and punching our fists at the sky may be the best way to deal with our pain. Neither our deep suffering nor our burning anger against the God we feel has ignored us is out of bounds, according to the Bible. In fact, this divine wrestling seems core to what a relationship with God looks like, according to these writers. A casual skimming of the book of Psalms should make it clear that nothing we feel is out of bounds. The ancient people who acknowledged that both God and suffering make up the foundation stones of life on earth were not confused by the explosions of pain and rage we feel. They who spent generations seeking God in the midst of slavery, oppression, violent loss, and common-to-all heartbreak are well positioned to teach us a way forward.

These mothers and fathers of our faith demonstrate how, through lament, we can catapult our fear, devastation, and blinding rage back on the Almighty. Hurl them. Let them fly. Martha, one of Jesus' closest friends, confronted Jesus to his face when her brother died (John 11:21-22). Jesus himself did this, amid the agony of the cross, calling out, "My God, my God, why have you forsaken me?" (Mark 15:34).

Jesus' words were well known to him and everyone listening, part of Psalm 22, which continues:

> Why are you so far from saving me,
>   so far from my cries of anguish?
> My God, I cry out by day, but you do not answer,
>   by night, but I find no rest. (Psalm 22:1-2)

Most of us who have been taught to expect suffering to play only a small role in our lives have not been taught how to leverage our raging, overpowering grief and anguish as the whip we sling at God—only to find that it becomes, over time, the rope holding us attached to God when we have long since lost the strength to hold on ourselves. But this is exactly what honest, anguished lament can be.

For Psalm 22 continues yet further. As the psalmist (and the community who use this psalm in their worship practices) continues his litany of grievances, the tone does eventually turn around. Bit by bit the psalmist remembers that God has proven faithful to generations, not in mitigating the realities of life on this earth but in continued presence:

> I will declare your name to my people;
>   in the assembly I will praise you.
> You who fear the Lord, praise him!
>   All you descendants of Jacob, honor him!
>   Revere him, all you descendants of Israel!
> For he has not despised or scorned
>   the suffering of the afflicted one;
> he has not hidden his face from him
>   but has listened to his cry for help. (Psalm 22:22-24)

For Jason, years of suffering caused his faith to tremble, caused him to question God's goodness and presence. And for Catherine, years of suffering finally (after a long, long time of trembling) convinced her that God is present, that God is good.

We don't get to choose which way our minds and hearts will take us, at first—if we'll approach this journey more like the fictional Peter or the fictional John in *The Chosen*. We won't know what the true fruit of our grief journey will be for years or decades down the road. Those who have survived the worst in life are typically too broken, too disoriented by the work of surviving to release hopeful press statements. It's far, far down the road when their voices can be heard.

Mary Oliver is a much-beloved poet who writes of the sacred-yet-simple delights of human life amid the natural world. Recently, a friend of Catherine's posted a wonder-struck poem of Oliver's on social media with a query for conversation: Is such an outlook, though lovely and inspiring, a bit naive? Could her simple joys be the fruit of comfort and privilege, an affront to those of us crashing against injustice and evil day after day after day?

The responses poured in immediately, links to articles and interviews Oliver gave throughout her life detailing her own great suffering. In 2011, Oliver shared publicly for the first time that she was neglected by her mother and sexually abused by her father.[3] Elsewhere she described her childhood as "very dark and broken."[4] To Krista Tippett she said, "It was a very bad childhood—for everybody, every member of the household, not just myself, I think—and I escaped it, barely, with years of trouble. But . . . I got saved by the beauty of the world."[5] Oliver survived decades of staring sorrow, death, and abject darkness in the face, and it was not in the absence of suffering but by finding a tunnel through these things that she gained the ability to speak so vividly of beauty and comfort, of glimpsing joy, of seeking delight. "What I have done," Mary Oliver once said, "is learn to love and learn to be loved. That didn't come easy. And I learned to consider my life an amazing gift."[6]

Casting our burdens on the one who calls himself "compassionate" (Psalm 86:15) and "close to the brokenhearted" (Psalm 34:18) will not remove our problems. God does not ever, ever promise that his followers will suffer less than any other creatures on this earth; in fact, Jesus promised his followers that they would suffer more (2 Timothy 3:12). Our pain will persist. Our questions will remain. Our crises of faith won't suddenly come to end.

But friend, we may learn how to draw near to the God who weeps, who suffers with us. In the mystery of it all, we may learn how to find Love.

IMMANUEL

In the months after Janae died, I (Jason) took long walks around my neighborhood. I sat down at picnic tables next to soccer fields and got to work on my catapult. There were so many volleys. Over and over I sent my accusations skyward. I had learned years before that these angry prayer sessions wouldn't make the pain stop, wouldn't answer any of my brokenhearted questions.

But as I practiced these brazen laments, I stopped doubting that God heard me. God can't ignore me that long, not when I'm shouting at the gate.

Eventually, I started to feel God's presence again, drawing close to me in my pain. And there, in those moments, I remembered that Jesus was named Immanuel: God with us. God next to us. God mourning alongside us. God helping us load up our siege engines for the next volley.

In his book *Letters from a Skeptic*, theologian Gregory A. Boyd writes of finding himself in a mid-faith crisis. Like so many before and after him, Boyd was overwhelmed by the unrelenting presence of suffering. How could the grandeur of the night sky and the fires of Auschwitz exist in the same universe? There must be a God, but how could there be a God? He wrote:

> I looked up at the sky and cried out with a loud, angry voice—"The only God I can believe in is one who knows firsthand what it's like to be a Jewish child buried alive, and knows what it's like to be a Jewish mother watching her child be buried!" And just then it occurred to me (or was it revealed?): That is exactly the kind of God Christianity proclaims.[7]

If you, like me, like Boyd, like untold others, have found your faith dying on the vine because suffering became too much to endure while proclaiming God's goodness and saving power, would you consider joining me on this bench in the park? We can sit together, cry together, scream and shout and throw things at the sky or into the dirt if we need to. In learning to practice honest, searing, anguished lament for all the evil and suffering and pain that piles up unrelentingly on our years of life, we find our best chance to surviving it all, and—as a great cloud of witnesses attest—our most honest chance of finding God's sustaining presence on this earth.

PRACTICE

||||||||||||||||||||||||||||||||||||||||||||||||||||||||||||||||||||||||||||||||||||||||||||||| *Lament*

If your faith began with a belief, even subtly, that God would shield you from the worst life has to offer, it's likely you've felt the sting of betrayal by now. If your mid-faith crisis included wrestling over the idea of a powerful God and a world filled with both beauty and pain, we invite you to join us in the spiritual practice of lament.

You don't need to find a bench in the park, but do select a space carefully. Start removing your grief and grievances from your mind and body, bit by bit. Depending on your temperament, this may take a few different forms. Perhaps you'll write them down, one by one. Perhaps you'll shout them aloud. You might want to draw them or collect pebbles in your hands to represent each one.

If you've found a way to represent them tangibly—by gathering pebbles or writing on paper—find a way to let them go. Bury them, burn them, or toss them into a river or lake (if you're using something organic). If you're using your voice, throw each one away from your body and toward God with your noise.

Don't hold back. You may be surprised by pain or emotions you weren't expecting, memories that surface, or resentments you didn't realize you felt. If you need support, don't hesitate to invite a friend to join you—or a trusted professional like a therapist, spiritual director, or pastor.

Finally, don't expect this to be a one-and-done experience. The ritual of removing long-buried words and feelings from your body will make an impact, but life is long and suffering is deep. Return to the practice of lament as often as necessary.

If and when your heart is ready, begin to incorporate a practice of gratitude as well. This may feel natural right away, or it may be years before this seems beneficial. Use a similar method of voicing, writing, or collecting each thing in your life for which you are genuinely grateful. These won't outweigh the losses and laments; life is such that they are intertwined. But over time, they may help you find a path forward.

Something to Listen To

- "The Road, the Rocks, and the Weeds," John Mark McMillan
- "Hold Me Jesus," Rich Mullins
- "Watch Over Us," The Lone Bellow

Something to Read

- *The Louder Song: Listening for Hope in the Midst of Lament*, Aubrey Sampson
- *All Shall Be Well: Awakening to God's Presence in His Messy, Abundant World*, Catherine McNiel
- *Aching Joy: Following God Through the Land of Unanswered Prayer*, Jason Hague

8

WHEN OUR BELIEFS COLLAPSED

Megan greeted me (Catherine) with a smile, a warm handshake, and eager eye contact as she offered me her seat. I accepted gratefully. Accompanying my son on a college visit, I felt far out of my depth; you never outgrow the awkwardness of visiting a new place that feels like home to everyone else. Booted from her normal spot, she chose a desk in the first row, right in front of the geology professor's lectern. Megan brought big Hermione Granger energy to this college classroom; it was evident she approached learning with the same bouncing eagerness she had shown me, a stranger old enough to be her mother.

This was a Christian college, and the topic (mostly over my non-geology-major head) had to do with the makeup of a particular layer of the earth's surface. But the class quickly sidetracked when the professor mentioned events dating back millions of years. The room became both quiet and restless simultaneously, as bodies shifted nervously in their chairs and ears perked up.

Fortunately, the professor was ready. He spent the next hour walking the class through various viewpoints people hold regarding the earth's origins, carefully outlining which were compatible with the Christian faith, which were compatible with scientific evidence—and which weren't. Young-earth creationism was on the list of possibilities for Christians, but it wasn't the only one, and it didn't make the scientifically feasible list. He gently yet firmly laid out the reality of what science shows us, what the Bible says, and various ways a faithful person might make sense of it all.

I was thrilled to see such thoughtful discipleship in action. But Megan in the front row was not. She asked question after question. It was clear that she trusted her professor both as a scientist and a Christian—but what he was telling her went against everything her family, her church community, and her faith-formation upbringing told her must be true if God was true, was real, was present.

Finally, she asked one last question. She paused for a long moment, found her shaking voice, and formed the words: "What about the flood?"

I saw her fears met and mirrored in the professor's tender voice and compassionate eyes as he answered, "There is no geological evidence for a worldwide flood."

Megan crumpled like a leaf.

I found myself wishing I could invite Megan to coffee, get to know her, and spend time listening to her thoughts and feelings after that class. I knew she was in good hands—the professor did not let her faith or feelings freefall but continued to walk her and the class through the good news of a faithful reading of the Bible that does not pit the Creator against creation or faith against science. It was evident he had been doing the dual work of pastor and scientist in this community of young learners for months and would not leave them to flounder no matter how long the journey took.

But I also knew a bit of how she felt. Almost thirty years earlier, I too sat in a geology classroom on my college campus. I too had been told by every single Christian I knew, every single person who had ever loved me, that in order for God and the Bible to be true and not a lie (and God's love, and a relationship with Jesus, and a life of faith, and heaven, and every single hope and comfort in this life and the next), then evolution had to be a lie. So, when I was faced with the evidence, I faced losing God forever. For us, this was the ultimate toggle switch, off or on, black or white. It was a setup, passed down to me unwittingly by every discipler and teacher I'd ever had.

Thankfully, my professor, too, taught real science without flinching. He gently, pastorally, listened to my questions as my worldview crumbled to the ground—and slowly, slowly was rebuilt from the rubble.

CUBICLE SCHOOL

I loved my small Christian elementary school. Friends and books and games in a cheerful environment, with my pastor-dad just down the hall? I had a blast.

My church followed the A.C.E. or Accelerated Christian Education model, a "Bible-based education for K-12," the current website reads.[1] We students—from first grade up through senior year—sat in little cubicles and taught ourselves from workbooks called PACEs. The curriculum was heavy on

things like seven-day creation (science), American exception-
alism (social studies), Bible memorization, and character
building. When we finished a unit, we raised a small American
flag into the air for permission to get up and score our work.
We'd walk to the center of the room in our past-the-knee skirts
(dress pants and ties for boys, ideally in red-white-and-blue),
compare our pages to the key, then walk back to our cubicle
for the next unit. If we did well, we got stickers. Accumulate
enough stickers, and we could choose a Jack Chick tract to add
to our collection. (Yes, really.) If we needed to use the restroom,
we raised a Christian flag instead.

I enjoyed myself so thoroughly that I had no idea any of this
was strange—until the year everything fell apart in my family
and I crash-landed into public junior high for seventh grade.
Even so, it wasn't until my college friends rolled on the floor
laughing at my depiction of what they called "cubicle school"
that it dawned on me how unusual my childhood had been.

But while few of us grew up in "cubicle school" waving
American flags when we had a question, many of us were
taught how to vigorously defend the Christian doctrines of our
communities, systems of thought that wove Bible stories and
principles throughout every aspect of modern life—but not
necessarily in a way that was biblically sound or informed by
a faithful, orthodox understanding of the Christian faith. Instead, much of it was rooted in an all-too-American ideology
that drew on biblical language and stories but had little to do
with the life of Christ and far more to do with American pol-
itics, narratives, culture wars, and control. The questions we
were measured against weren't about the divinity of Christ and

his death and resurrection, whether we loved our neighbors as we loved ourselves, what steps we took to love and forgive our enemies, how we as a community could give all we had to care for the poor (all things Jesus taught his followers were necessary to follow him). In fact, we rarely talked about historic Christian teachings at all. Of paramount importance were questions of this sort: Do you believe in a literal seven-day creation? Can you identify which American political party is "godly" versus "godless"? Do you know how the world will end, and what the end times will look like? Which news sources do you believe?

What mattered was that we understood these questions had a clear right and wrong answer—we were right and they were wrong—and that this was paramount not only for remaining securely within the community but also for remaining within the faith. It was God's clear teaching in the Bible that led us here. Any deviation or exploration could result in disaster.

But, by design, we didn't really feel the threat. This sort of closed community overflows with warmth and acceptance for those on the inside. There is a powerful sense of belonging, not only to the people around you but to a ready-made community of believers around the world. Why would we question or consider other perspectives when the stakes were as high as life and death, God and godlessness, heaven and hell—and we already had the right answers? When we already had God?

This is the How It Started of faith for many of us: a safe and secure home in a community we belonged in, one that provided all the answers to any questions we had. The right answers too, and a sense of identity as God's people, the faithful ones, beloved ones.

But sometimes we go out into the world and learn stuff that just doesn't fit this worldview. Sometimes even when we read the Bible, we find things that don't fit this worldview, or we discover things about our community itself that make us wonder. There are cracks, gaps, questions. We meet new people or encounter different ideas and find that, as warned, they are compelling.

That's what happened to Megan that morning I visited her geology class. When it comes, this moment hits like devastation, the beginning of the end—if not the atomic bomb that decimates everything in one fell swoop, without warning. One woman posted on an online forum: "I grew up on this stuff. I was so brainwashed. When I learned actual history in high school and college, my religious views had to crumble. It was traumatic and hurtful. And no one paid attention."

JOHN AND SOPHIA

Catherine met John and Sophia at a theology conference outside Chicago. They were in their midthirties, married, and had just left the church that had been their home for their entire lives. Their last ten years had been one long mid-faith crisis.

For as long as they could remember, John and Sophia had faithfully and joyfully attended church three times a week next to their parents, grandparents, aunts, uncles, and cousins. They planned to raise their own children here, too, alongside friends who enjoyed the same multigenerational support. Church was family literally and figuratively, a beautiful reflection of how Jesus intended this body to function. Children stayed in the Sunday services with the grownups, and everyone stayed after church for potlucks. And in the summertime, they all packed up their backpacks and bedrolls and went to camp together, where they enjoyed crystal-clear swimming lakes, Scripture songs, and the beauty of God's creation.

But as they entered adulthood, Sophia became uneasy about some of the church's teachings. "In our church, having the right answer was a moral issue, no matter what the question," she told me. "Nothing was amoral. And that got complicated, because we had some unique beliefs that few other Christians have, like the instrument thing."

The instrument thing was really a no-instrument thing: this church didn't allow musical instruments of any kind. The only music allowed in worship was a cappella, and drumming was off limits too.

This doctrine is not unheard of, and it's not new. Various Christian groups have embraced an instrument-free philosophy over the centuries, but this local group paired the teaching with a fervor that naturally led to alienation. This, and several other fundamentals, weren't just personal convictions or matters of conscience for this congregation but a badge of identity, a sign that they were right when so many others were wrong.

This got personal for John. He was naturally inclined to love melody and rhythm, eagerly joining band with the rest of his school classmates in fifth grade. He had real talent as a drummer, and since the class took place during school hours, he didn't think anything of it—he just went along to music class with everyone else. His parents didn't mind—but they didn't really discuss it either. By the time he was in high school, he had been marked as one of the top performers and was recruited by the town's marching band drumline. Playing for parades and football games would not have violated the rules, technically. Playing at school events was not the same as worshiping in his church sanctuary. But while his parents were hesitantly willing to sign the form, he knew many of his relatives would frown on such a public display, and his pastor definitely wouldn't approve.

"It was a huge sacrifice for him," Sophia said. "His closest friends were part of the band, and they couldn't understand why he dropped out. He was just trying to do what was right in the eyes of God, but he missed out on some incredible opportunities. He's always wished he could have had those memories, that team experience throughout high school, the chance to grow and explore being a musician."

Watching John wrestle raised questions for Sophia that nagged at her for years afterward. "I started studying the Bible more deeply, and I couldn't find anything that indicated God thought musical instruments were bad—not at all. We were insisting on this idea, this supposedly key thing that set us apart, based entirely on assumption or tradition. I kept wondering, 'Why are we equating this cultural belief with belief in God?'"

This line of thinking was unsettling and felt dangerous. Just as she had been warned, reconsidering one doctrine was a slippery slope. For months, questions swirled around her. If her church had been wrong about this, what else had they been wrong about? More, how could studying the Bible—the act of faithfulness and devotion she had been taught to pursue with all her mind and heart—be the thing that shook her faith?

"She was really distressed," John remembers. "And to be clear, it wasn't about music. It was about belonging. In our church, there was this unspoken understanding: 'you belong with us because you believe with us.' Which was amazing. But if you stopped believing what 'we' believe, you didn't belong anymore. And that was terrifying."

John was content with the sacrifice he had made—but the pain of it came roaring back years later when the church began teaching that the only candidate a Christian could vote for in the upcoming presidential election was someone he considered morally bankrupt. "This was the last straw for me. It seemed that every aspect of our lives was given moral weight as a litmus test on whether we belonged. But was the basis of morality actually God's law and Jesus' teaching as they claimed? I wasn't allowed to play the drums because it was viewed as a sin—but this candidate bragged about sexually assaulting women, and we were supposed to support him?"

Eventually, neither John nor Sophia could honestly say they trusted their church—their lifelong home, their extended family, their people. But at the same time, they didn't dare speak this out loud. The stakes were too high. They were repulsed, but afraid. Was their faith evaporating? Were they turning away from God? Were they being deceived? Was there any way to keep their place in the family if they were found out? Hiding felt like their only option.

"I would go to church and sing with a big smile on my face," Sophia remembers. "But inside, I was imploding. I didn't dare tell anyone what was going on behind my smile. Because if they knew I was no longer in agreement on so many things, I wouldn't be seen as one of them anymore. Worse, I would be seen as a threat, as unfaithful to God and a source of temptation. If I lost my church community, what would be left? Our mental health was suffering by staying, but I knew that if we left, it would suffer in a whole new way—and we would really hurt people we loved."

The final decision came a few years later during the church's annual meeting. John and Sophia came wearing masks, per local Covid-19 instructions. They were greeted in the foyer and told they had to remove the masks to enter. They were devastated, not only by the demand but by the lack of compassion being offered. Sophia had lost a cousin to Covid-19 just a month before, and they were both reeling with grief and loss. If the rest of the church didn't want to mask, that was one thing. But to callously demand that they take theirs off?

In this terrible, painful moment of clarity, a sense of peace settled over them both. "We just knew. This was it; we were done," John recalls. "We would submit to their wishes this last time, and then we would go."

Indeed, it was the last time. But though it was a gift to finally have clarity, the loss cut deep. For three days, Sophia stayed in her bed and wept for all they had left behind and all that was still unknown.

A COMMON TALE

John and Sophia have an extreme story, but a common one. Millions of us face a devastating faith crisis when the teachings of our communities—doctrines that are not actually part of the historic Christian faith as we were taught—are proven false. When you're taught that God's love, relationship, and even existence must be paired with a series of unrelated cultural beliefs, the stakes are high, for who wants to lose God over a spot in the marching band or a good grade in a science class? When your identity is deeply rooted in a community that emphasizes being right as necessary for God's existence and your salvation, any conflicting idea is seen as a threat— and so will you be, if you consider them.

For those of us who grew up in this environment, a mid-faith crisis is almost inevitable. Either we discover a whiff of goodness and truth outside the safety ropes, or we find flaws and falsehood inside it. And when one (or both) of those things happens, we find ourselves staring into a terrifying vacuum.

But is that slippery slope a nefarious temptation away from truth, God, and faith—or the next step on our journey of faith, toward God and truth?

We're left reeling, afraid. If we tell the truth of what we think and know, what we've seen, we risk losing everything— including ourselves. Including God. But we can't keep on living a lie. We're disoriented, disillusioned, hurt, and angry. Eventually, the weight of cognitive dissonance and fear becomes too much, and we turn away.

This is the tragic end of the false choice we were offered at the very beginning, the fruit of the seed that was planted. It is paramount that we learn a new way, a truer path for ourselves and those who come behind us.

While he was on earth, living out each day with his friends, Jesus said that his followers would be known by their love (John 13:35). And in fact, he tended to avoid those who considered themselves knowledgeable experts about things of God, venturing instead toward those who were confused, searching, questioning, rejected, entirely lost. When he did converse with the know-it-alls, he tended to make them angry (angry enough that they killed him), declaring that their systems would be torn down and replaced, that those at the very edges of "rightness" would enter the kingdom of God ahead of them (Matthew 21:31).

In the decades and centuries after his death, the early Christians concluded that we should agree on a few important things: that Jesus was the Christ, the Son of God; that he was killed but God raised him from the dead; that he would return again to defeat evil once and for all. And, in the meantime, we were to continue his mission of loving God and loving each other, along with the Spirit and the church, following the teachings he gave while on earth.

After that, it got complicated. Very complicated, very fast. Disagreements resulted in doctrines that resulted in rules that resulted in more disagreements. It's been a long, long time since Christians were known primarily for our love—long since we even thought to aim for such a goal. For centuries now we've spilled blood and sacrificed relationships to ensure we are known as those who hold the right doctrines and know the right answers. We've defended a particular worldview rather than defending the hurting and lost. Holding the line became more important than loving even family. Angrily fighting those with whom we disagree became more important than spreading compassion and provision for those in desperate need.

There's a hand-drawn comic that demonstrates this, featuring a church membership class. Front and center is a projector screen detailing the endless divisions of the Christian faith over time. On the left a small dot represents Jesus and his followers. Then, the dot splits off into bullet points, which split into more bullet points until the entire screen is filled with countless brackets and notches representing the diverse array of Christian expression around the world and through the centuries. The teacher points to the right side of the screen, where one of the tiny notches is circled.

"So this is where our movement came along and got the Bible right," he says. A smiling student chirps, "Jesus is so lucky to have us!"[2]

They say that much truth is said in jest, and this cartoon puts us all in our place. No matter what theology we ascribe to, no matter what Christian expression we find most affinity with, we have to admit our perspective is one of many. That's not a bad thing, friend—not frightening or dangerous—because, once again, while we are seekers of truth, our faith is not rooted in our rightness. The Christian heritage includes a rich tapestry of diverse thought and practice as followers of Jesus have tried their best to understand who God is, what Jesus wants, what Scripture means, and how to apply it over two thousand years in countless cultures and time periods. We have arrived at a myriad of different conclusions. Some have kept Jesus and his teaching in the center well, and some have done it poorly. Most have had mixed results. But still, we remain brothers and sisters—so long as we are known for our love.

We have at our disposal a huge legacy from every century and continent, women and men who worshiped with different postures and rituals, who emphasized some doctrines over others, who engaged with culture in vastly different ways. Some lit candles and sat in silence, some sang praise songs a cappella, and some played hymns on pianos in local pubs. They even held different interpretations about the creation of the world, the end of the world, and the best way to live in the world in the meantime.

The one thing we all have in common is Jesus at the center.

WHERE WE GO FROM HERE

John and Sophia realized they had three choices: stay where they were in the dissonance, living a double life; leave their community, faith, and God entirely; or search out a path that led toward an understanding of God they could embrace while attempting to maintain their relationships. They chose the third path—and it has not been easy.

The temptation is to find a new tribe with just as rigid a worldview, with litmus tests just as damning—but at a different place on the theological and ideological spectrum. But importantly, urgently, if we are to move toward health and truth, we must resist the temptation to create a new set of ultimatums. We don't grow by moving from the right to the left, or vice versa, retaining our fundamentalist zeal for a different worldview. We grow by pursuing wisdom and humility, by learning to sit comfortably with mystery.

Though we were implicitly taught otherwise, we cannot earn love—or salvation—by rightness. We are not even asked to defend or prove God's existence by rightness, for Jesus said that the proof would be in our love. The invitation before us is to walk away from formulaic narratives and into a more robust, mature story. Our destination isn't a new set of precepts and certainties, a new definition of who is "in" and who is "out." Our destination is more expansive than that, more life giving, and much more challenging to get to: resting in the love of God without having all the answers—or, possibly, any of the answers. We are infants in God's arms, and he has never asked us to transcend our mortal limits and attain omniscience or perfection.

But to do this, we need to quiet our screaming nervous systems. Everything in how we are wired pushes against this, desperate for the right answer, the certain path, the proof we are the ones who have it right, the ones who are accepted on the merit of our rightness. How do we learn to rest in unknowing, in mystery, in trust that God never claimed to judge us based on how well we score on a doctrinal test?

We have high hopes for Megan, even as her world and faith crumbled in her geology classroom, because—as Catherine experienced, thirty years earlier—she has a shepherd, a pastoral guide who understands the false choice she was presented with in her formative years and all it means for her now. She has an entire community around her who are dedicated to searching for God's truth in the Bible, and in the water tables, soil samples, and jet-stream patterns, who approach apparent contradictions with curiosity and humility, not pridefulness and fear.

Though the process itself felt like death, John and Sophia found new life when they walked away. After the spinning in pain and confusion began to quiet, they dipped their toes in a church where they knew a few people. They lay low, flying under the radar, taking it all in—then committed to attending regularly. They didn't start serving or volunteering, even though they had always been in leadership before. But they joined a home group with hopes of becoming known, and sat in Sunday services, receiving.

The church they found has instruments, guitars, keyboards, drums. The worship and theology feel strange at times, and they don't always agree with the pastor. It isn't perfect. But the people they met demonstrate to them the patient, accepting love of Jesus that does not ask us to figure everything out before we can be included, before we can be loved.

Friend, if your ability to think and believe rightly was given the power to determine God's love for you or even God's existence, the difference between an eternity of joy versus torture, or if you could remain in relationship with your family and friends, then you will reasonably experience panic at the thought of leaving behind ideas you can no longer believe. You may feel an urgency to find a new all-powerful truth and cling to that instead. That's reasonable and understandable. That is how many of our brains were wired, and we can hardly imagine feeling soothed and calm without that.

May we invite you to take a deep breath and learn, bit by bit, step by step, to let go of such high-stakes thinking? Ultimatums like these take a toll on your mind and heart and will not ultimately increase your odds of finding truth. Instead, our prayer and hope are that you will find peace and rest in the mystery of God's love and being. We pray that, like Megan, John, and Sophia, you will find faithful guides who will lead you not to another tribe from whence you can look haughtily down on a new group of people who are wrong—but to a deeply committed, curious, and humble faith. A place where you can pray with the psalmist:

My heart is not proud, Lord,
 my eyes are not haughty;
I do not concern myself with great matters
 or things too wonderful for me.
But I have calmed and quieted myself,
 I am like a weaned child with its mother;
 like a weaned child I am content. (Psalm 131:1-2)

Take a deep, deep breath, friend. You are loved with an everlasting love.

PRACTICE

‖‖ *Finding Mercy in Mystery*

If your mid-faith crisis included confronting black-and-white thinking you were taught was necessary for a life of faith, it's possible you don't quite know what to believe anymore. This can be terrifying. When our sense of worth (not to mention eternal destiny) has been directly linked to our belief in right doctrines, letting go of these doctrines, without new "rightness" to take their place, can launch real anxiety. It may be all but impossible to be still and quiet your soul.

One place we might begin is with the prayer of the blind man, Bartimaeus. When Jesus passed by, he shouted, "Jesus, Son of David, have mercy on me!" (Mark 10:47). That simple utterance of desperation has become a sacred starting place for millions of Christians over the centuries. This plea has taken on countless variations as men and women find themselves drawn to the prayer's desperate humility, its direct address of Jesus. In the Eastern Orthodox Church, these words have become known as the Jesus Prayer, and are usually adapted like this: "Lord Jesus Christ, Son of God, have mercy on me, a sinner." As we learn to come to Jesus without first proving we can pass a true/false exam, this prayer may be a helpful starting place for us too.

Find a quiet place. You can be sitting or walking or doing anything really, but for this practice you may want to try kneeling, to express the posture of surrender. We are releasing our desire to have the answers, letting go of the message that we must earn our approval from God by passing a test. Instead, as trusting children quiet and stilled, we prepare to receive love and mercy without strings attached.

Begin with a moment of silence. Breathe deeply and slowly. Then, in God's presence, let the questions that paralyze you come to mind. Let the fears that accompany those questions come to mind. Hold your hands out as if you are holding each of those precious burdens, allowing them to fall to the floor at God's feet.

As you breathe in, pray the first words of the prayer. As you breathe out, pray the final words. Find a cadence in which the words fit into the flow of your slow, deep breathing. In this way, you can bring this prayer with you wherever you go, calming your body and mind. You can whisper the prayer, or you can cry out, like Bartimaeus: "Lord Jesus Christ, Son of God, have mercy on me!"

Of course, there is nothing magical about this prayer, but it can be a wonderful invitation. We can breathe these words all day long, if needed, receiving God's love and care when we are right, and when we are wrong, without fear.

Something to Listen To

- "Psalm 131," Poor Bishop Hooper
- "I Don't Know Anything," John Mark Pantana

Something to Read

- *Fearing Bravely: Risking Love for Our Neighbors, Strangers, and Enemies*, Catherine McNiel
- *Faith Unraveled: How a Girl Who Knew All the Answers Learned to Ask Questions*, Rachel Held Evans
- *The Sin of Certainty: Why God Desires Our Trust More Than Our "Correct" Beliefs*, Peter Enns

9

WHEN FEELINGS FADED

My (Catherine's) early childhood Sunday school classes were held in a musty basement, child-size chairs temporarily filling the space that would later host the afternoon potluck. Before asking us to sit quietly for the lesson, our teachers would lead us in full-body action songs so we could get our wiggles out. They held up faded posterboards with the lyrics, one stanza per sheet, words playfully interspersed with pictures for those still learning to read. We knew exactly when to jump up, jump down, or wave our arms in the air.

One song was especially fun, each sheet of posterboard covered with images of brightly colored fruit and candy to represent the lyrics to a song called "Apple-Red Happiness."[1] We sang loudly, declaring that giving our lives to God would result in things like popcorn energy and gummy bear cheerfulness; that life with Jesus would be one long candy-filled holiday. The benefits of life with Jesus, the lyrics promised, were "super satisfying." All we had to do was try it, and we would see how sweet and exciting our lives became.

Before we were old enough to read, we knew for sure that life with Jesus would always be happiness "inside, outside, upside, downside." He had come in, cleansed our hearts from sin, and now we had "The joy, joy, joy, joy down in our hearts. Where? Down in our hearts to stay!"[2]

Looking back, I can't fault my Sunday school teachers. They weren't theologians but dairy farmers, volunteering their time to nurture us kids in the best way they knew how. But I would have preferred more honest marketing about the Christian life, a more authentic invitation to discipleship. To paraphrase Michael Scott of *The Office*,[3] while Sunday school teachers made a lot of false promises in their day, this one was the most generous: Follow Jesus, and feel good all the time. Not just good, but great! One long gummy worm holiday. This was our destiny because we loved Jesus and Jesus loved us so very much.

What could go wrong?

The candy-coated faith of our elementary Sunday school days shifted to pep-rally faith in our teens and twenties. We traded musty basements for exciting regional conferences or massive national gatherings, our idealistic young adult minds and hearts whipped up into a frenzy of missional zeal and spiritual euphoria. At Christian camp, conferences, or college we were lit on fire. We discovered what we'd been looking for, found the secret. One popular young adult ministry adopted "I Found It!" as their marketing slogan. We attended rallies named "Acquire the Fire," were invited to "Mountaintop Experiences," and became "Radically Saved." We were assured that this was just the beginning, that great things were in store if we stayed faithful to God and God's plan for our lives. We were "great big bundles of potentiality" pumped up with louder and louder shouts insisting that this joy, this peace, this powerful sense of identity and meaning was the most real thing, and it was ours now, forever.

Just like that.

THE LETDOWN

The truth is, following God is not a one-way ticket to the mountaintop, and it never has been. No one can camp at the summit for long. Research bears out what we learned the hard way: religious experiences do create feelings of euphoria. So does falling in love, experimenting with drugs, or completing a marathon. But our nervous systems are not created to sustain that level of emotion. None of us can, not under any circumstance. We may spend a lifetime chasing that deep sense of well-being, but we simply are not wired to experience those emotions full time. No matter what we do to seek euphoria, the joy, joy, joy, joy down in our hearts is not here to stay.

We've already looked at the myth of faith as a shield against suffering, illness, and death—but there's a second layer, a more vulnerable layer: our longing to feel that everything is okay, that we're okay. We trusted that God was by our side always, that we would always *feel* him there. We would suffer in this life, but with Jesus we had everything we needed to make it through. We believed it, and not just in a transactional way: we trusted him. We believed in the person, the God we had all but fallen in love with, trusted that these euphoric feelings would never let us down because he would never let us down.

But after a few dozen trips around the sun, most of us have encountered a different truth: God's emotional benefits are occasionally stingier than we expected. We don't feel everything we want to feel. Not at all. We're stressed out and exhausted. We are beaten down and numb. We're on edge. The fruit of the Spirit seems increasingly hard to come by. Most of us didn't ask God for wealth, prosperity, or popularity. We knew that wasn't in the contract, but we were counting on love, joy, peace, patience, kindness, goodness, faithfulness, gentleness, and self-control. In reality, we catch glimpses of God's presence, sometimes, maybe. But there's rarely any double-fudge fulfillment to be found.

The crisis slips in slowly and takes a seat, sitting quietly for months or even years before we notice it's there. If Jesus were truly enough, why do we still feel emptiness? If the benefits of his love were super satisfying (as my childhood song promised), why do we feel decidedly unsatisfied?

The promises we clung to did not hold up, and so we're left wondering, "Where did God go? Was God ever really there in the first place, or did we just imagine it?"

We can fake it, of course. We can hold onto the veneer of "I'm doing great! Victory in Jesus!" We can learn how to put on a holy smile, show a falsely perfect self, marriage, family, and general dream-come-true reality to the Christian world. If we don't, they'll know we're unworthy.

But by putting on this mask, we lose our last great hope of finding something real, something that could turn us toward lasting peace and well-being: we traded the experience of being known and loved by a community for the hope of being tolerated by a community because they like our false happy smile.

If we build our faith on spiritual euphoria and hope for a rock-solid sense of well-being, the walls crumble quickly. "I don't feel God at all," we say, and with this declaration comes a sense that we've been abandoned, or that we were tricked into opening our eager hearts.

For there is a darkness so dark no light can be seen to penetrate it.

Jason's friends Jim and Kelly watched a terrible, fast-moving cancer take their precious, faithful mother's life. And while they never demanded that God heal her, they did ask God to grant her peace. Instead, they witnessed her spirit suffer as much trauma as her body, the darkness and despair growing and prevailing through to the very last moment.

Experiences like these are hard to recover from, and they leave us on our knees surrounded by questions we cannot answer. If God is near in the hard times, why can't we feel him? If God's comforting presence is not perceivable in the valley of the shadow of death, what has this all been about?

MY MID-FAITH MOM

You know that "Apple-Red Happiness" song? While we kids shouted our hearts out with caramel cheerfulness and pomegranate praise, my (Catherine's) mid-faith mom was fighting back. She abhorred the song and wanted to find more truthful options. She herself battled clinical depression, but this was the 1980s. Society didn't understand mental health issues, but the church lagged even further behind, viewing these illnesses as spiritual failure. Just pray more. Have more faith. Let the sweetness carry you away.

My mother was raised in an emotionally abusive family, and she came to adulthood not at all certain that she was loved, that her life had value, that she was worth anything at all. Meeting Jesus in her early twenties genuinely changed everything. For the first time, she heard and believed she was created on purpose, out of love—that she was known, that she was precious, that she was valued. She believed there was a God she could follow, a community she could join, a love she could know and be known by. This life-changing good news changed her entire trajectory: who she married and how she raised her children, where she lived and what she did for a living. The gospel—the good news—changed her forever, cementing her in a faith family, offering her truth, and providing the courage to repeat that truth over the haunting voices of condemnation.

If anyone could out-faith depression, it would have been her. She was a rule follower, and she followed all the rules. Yet, while she would be the first to testify that God's great love was super satisfying, giving Christ her life resulted in neither apple-red happiness nor gummy-bear cheerfulness, and certainly not sugary singing inside.

Thankfully, my mother found helpful guides who taught her that depression was not rooted in spiritual failures. Her lack of euphoria wasn't a sign that Jesus had left her, or proof that God was somehow displeased. Thanks to a pioneering doctor she listened to on her kitchen FM radio, she defied the Christian norms of the day by seeking treatment. She began seeing a psychologist and taking antidepressants years before the stigma of such things began to fade.

We're not all suffering from depression like my mom, but many of us have mistakenly jumped to spiritual conclusions regarding our emotional experiences. We've felt a cold distance from the God who used to feel closer than a brother. We've felt lostness or numbness and thought God might have really left us. We thought we made a big mistake somewhere along the line, or that we were currently doing something wrong to drive the Holy Spirit away. But just like my mom's case, there are other causes for our emotional ups and downs, and there are better ways to understand them.

DESOLATION AND CONSOLATION

It should be clear by now that crises of faith are normal and even necessary steps on the journey to spiritual maturity, but they are not fun, not easy to survive. The mid-faith crisis of desolation seems particularly abundant, even (and perhaps especially) common in the people we extol as saints or grandparents in the faith. If we look past our culture's recent spiritual mythologies, sugar-coated Christian novels, and "safe for the whole family" media, we find a similar story playing out over and over again on our long journeys of faith.

For centuries, Christian seekers viewed emotional and spiritual distress not as proof of God's absence or our failure but as a pathway to God, lights lighting the road in the darkness, pointing us back home. The mystics surmised that our internal battles were trails leading to a closer identification with Jesus, the death throes of our sinful nature, and the doorway to newness of life and greater spiritual maturity. They believed that seasons, even long seasons, of spiritual darkness and disorientation could be forerunners to increased insight and unity with God, with the Spirit. They believed that difficult years of struggle, not joyful years of spiritual ease, would result in fruit.

They believed these emotions were given to us not because God is punishing or abandoning us but simply because the road of life is steep and harrowing. And from within these roiling emotions, God is gently, eagerly, persistently calling us. But we need help in order to see this, to interpret it and find a path forward.

Saint Ignatius of Loyola, a sixteenth-century Spanish priest and theologian, introduced language that has helped millions of Catholic and Protestant Christians find that path. Ignatius talked of consolation and desolation, which he said were movements of the soul—or, we might say, the pathway your soul is on at any given moment. *Consolation* he defined as a movement toward "hope, faith and charity, and all interior joy which calls and attracts to heavenly things and to the salvation of one's soul, quieting it and giving it peace in its Creator and Lord."[4] *Desolation*, by contrast, is a disturbance in the soul, a "movement to things low and earthly, the unquiet of different agitations and temptations, moving to want of confidence, without hope, without love, when one finds oneself all lazy, tepid, sad, and as if separated from his Creator and Lord."[5]

There's value in describing these opposites not as set-in-stone descriptors of a person's inner state but as movements, like the movements in a symphony. They don't last forever, often repeat, and often overlap. They flow in ways that are surprising and unpredictable. Like a symphony, both the jubilant movements and the mournful movements are necessary to produce anything of lasting depth or beauty. If we are on any kind of spiritual journey, we will encounter a good mix of both.

Earlier we talked about Mother Teresa's intense, private struggle with doubt. In her journals and letters, she goes further, describing her long season of spiritual desolation in stark, almost chilling terms. "There is so much contradiction in my soul. Such deep longing for God, so deep that it is painful. A suffering continual. And yet not wanted by God. Repulsed. Empty. No faith, no love, no zeal." "Within me, everything is icy cold."[6]

She did not write these words in a season of failure. Her Sisters of Charity were experiencing a season of remarkable fruitfulness in Calcutta. They were loving well, serving the bodies and souls of the poor and afflicted. They were being like Jesus. And yet, she says, "There is such a deep loneliness in my heart. . . . How long will our Lord stay away?"

"I want to smile even at Jesus and so hide, if possible, the pain and darkness of my soul, even from him."[7]

Saint John of the Cross would have understood her pain. He battled profound levels of spiritual doubt and turmoil. A priest, mystic, and friar who wrote poetry and commentary on spiritual darkness and crisis, John is best known to us as the author of *Dark Night of the Soul*. He described this as an experience where doubt and anguish are the necessary process of our souls dying to themselves, being freed to finally arrive in the sweetness of God's presence. And while he envisioned the ultimate destination to be the soul's union with God, he believed one of the final stops along the way was a deep faith crisis—a sense of God's complete absence, an inability to register God's presence at all. And along with it, a sense of confusion and spiritual stagnation, discouragement, and despair.

But as we so often like to say, John's point was that the darkest hour comes before dawn. Marathon runners talk about "hitting a wall" twenty miles or so through their race, the "dark time" where they face the toughest physical and mental battle to continue. And yet, all who have finished the race know that strength is found to go on. A woman laboring in childbirth goes through the most harrowing stage, called "the transition stage," when she often wants to give up so profoundly that death no longer seems the worse option. And yet, this sense of despair is a sure indication that her labors are nearly finished, new life right around the corner.

In other words, your emotional or spiritual low points may not signify God's absence or your failure at all; they may be part of the ups and downs of life, signs that your spirit is preparing for a time of growth and fulfillment as the dormancy of winter readies the ground for spring. Not only is desolation, and the faith crisis that goes with it, not a sure sign of the death of your faith, but it may lead you, slowly but surely, toward consolation.

We're not suggesting the change will come quickly or easily. If Mother Teresa struggled for so long, we too might wrestle desolation through long seasons. The invitation, however, is a real one—and it is this invitation that so changed my mother's life.

Like all of us, she still walks through valleys of desolation. But she leans toward consolation, even before she has it. When she cannot see or feel God's presence, she repeats the words on the three-by-five cards taped all around the house: Do not fear for I am with you. Do not be dismayed for I am your God. I will strengthen you. I will help you. I will uphold you with my mighty right hand.

And in this way, she is upheld.

My mother's testimony—and the testimony of thousands of spiritual seekers before her—is that God is present when we cannot see or feel him, even during the darkest nights, within our deepest crises of faith.

But to be lifted up, often we have to let go. For when the tsunami comes, it is not the brick walls that survive but that which can release and float—not what tries to stand firm but what is able to surrender. As my ocean-lifeguard husband reminds us each time we go to the beach, swimming with all your might against a rip tide is a nearly certain path to death. This hard work, this life-and-death effort to survive is, ironically, the very thing that will kill you. The rip tide will carry you further and further out to sea until you become exhausted and finally succumb. But if you instead let go, stop swimming, and simply float for a while, you can paddle a short distance parallel to the shore and escape the current.

Friend, sometimes this is the invitation found in spiritual crisis too: what will survive is what can release. The brick wall feels stronger, but it will be toppled. Rather than standing strong against the tides of dark emotion and doubt, what if we let go?

The surprise ending is that just maybe we will be upheld, not entirely swept away by these currents of despair.

CLOUD OF WITNESSES

Back when I (Jason) was a kid, performing spiritually euphoric Jesus songs with two dozen other exuberant children, we had one song that was different from the others. It always made the old people cry, and it went like this:

> More faithful than the sun to rise,
>> the stars to shine, the seasons change.
> You are, You are.

What made this song noticeably different was the complete lack of choreography. There were no dance moves, and no hand motions. Instead, we were encouraged to "enter into worship" by raising our hands to God if we felt the pull. And I always felt the pull. The words of the chorus would sweep me away, and I would squeeze my eyes shut and stretch my arms wide.

> You are faithful, Lord, never wavering Guide,
> Unending source, ageless Creator.
> You are faithful, Lord![8]

When I opened my eyes, I'd see tears slipping down the cheeks of the old folks, mirroring back the emotion we felt in our own hearts.

In those moments, I wasn't performing. I really did feel it— the rush of holy love starting in my belly and spreading outward to my hands and feet. I might have been young, and yes, I was probably playing to the crowd a bit, but I *knew* God was faithful, and I believed God would always be faithful. And that by *faithful* we meant present in a way we could sense in our inner beings. If times got dark and the feelings got stale, I could lift my hands and the euphoria would return.

Of course, I was just a kid. I knew nothing of the years of spiritual desolation that were sure to follow; it all sounded easy back then. But it hits me looking back on that memory that this naivete wasn't true for the "grand-saints" who watched our worship and cried. Most of them lived through one or even both world wars, Korea, Vietnam. They were drafted, or fought, or were left behind, or lost those they loved. They survived the Great Depression, the fight for civil rights, and so much more. They lost children or spouses to illness and accidents. Surely, they encountered dark nights of the soul, crises of faith, and seasons of desolation. But they made it out alive. They found consolation, deep and living, and in the process they gained the tools to find the way back again and again, in the darkest night. After all they had seen and survived, their summary report for the younger generation was this: God has been faithful.

Many of us seem to believe that the fruits of the Spirit—like salvation—are free gifts from God. We assume love, joy, peace, patience, and the rest come as a free download when we sign up to receive mail from the Spirit. When we find ourselves profoundly lacking every one of these desperately needed resources in our moment of crisis, we can't make sense of it— unless faith and God's promises have all been a sham, a phishing scheme.

But there is that great cloud of witnesses behind us, our now-departed grandparents in the faith along with the saints and mystics of old, declaring that after decades of reaching toward God in the darkness, they eventually found that God had been faithful to them all along.

TRAVELING COMPANIONS

If we're going to find a path forward from this faith crisis, we need to readjust our expectations. Neither How It Started nor How It's Going is a true snapshot of what life has to offer. What we were taught—or at least, what we believed—was too simple a picture. Faith is not an easy stroll along the mountaintop with God at our side. The joy, joy, joy we feel on a good day is not here to stay. But neither should we expect the reverse: white knuckling, digging deep, not letting our true pain show lest we lose our spiritual credibility. The path forward may not have been outlined in Sunday school, but the grandfathers and grandmothers of our faith know it well. Their lives and testimonies demonstrate that life is hard, that euphoria is fleeting, and even a sense of well-being is hard to come by. And yet, now that they have nearly completed the journey and have a moment to turn around, they declare with genuine conviction that God was with them all the way because they never stopped reaching out.

Though it was likely missing from the American traditions that launched our pursuit of faith and happiness, the Ignatian ideas of spiritual desolation and spiritual consolation help us remember to lift our hands. While desolation turns us inward, toward ourselves and away from community, draining our energy and driving ourselves down a spiral of negative feelings, consolation directs our senses back to God and back to community, moving our focus away from ourselves. If we desire consolation, we shouldn't just wait for it to arrive; we should lean toward relationships.

In my own bouts with depression, I (Jason) have felt the pull to isolate. Whenever I do, I lose perspective, and despair piles on despair. Thankfully, I have learned to let other people into my life to help me navigate this journey. For the spiritual life is indeed a wilderness journey, and we will not survive it on our own. We need wise friends, honest and authentic traveling companions who can nudge us back to health and point out ways God may be speaking to us out of the darkness.

The gift of being honest and truthful with spiritual companions requires a level of true vulnerability and trustworthiness, but the benefits are more than worth it. I have several people in my life who know me intimately. They know my longings and my brokenness, my deepest prayers and my worst corruptions, and yet they still love me. When I share updates on my spiritual journey with them, they lean in. They listen. And they help me see things I didn't see before. In their company, I find the gentle tug toward consolation, and I know that I am not alone. Christ is with me, even if I can only feel his presence through my companions.

Maybe you already have spiritual companions in your life and don't need to go any further. Or maybe, like me, you feel the need for extra help in discerning your life with God. If that's the case, I'd like to introduce the practice of spiritual direction.

Spiritual direction is another foundational component of Ignatian spirituality, and one that a growing number of Catholics and Protestants alike have found life giving and spiritually nourishing. As the name implies, this practice is all about trajectory, for spiritual direction is "a relationship that is going somewhere. God is leading the person to deeper faith and more generous service. The spiritual director asks not just 'what is happening?' but 'what is moving forward?'"[9] In this relationship, we meet with a director much as we would a therapist or counselor, in weekly or monthly or occasional meetings. But rather than dispensing advice, the spiritual director listens—not only to us as we share what is on our minds but also to the Spirit as hints of God's movement are revealed in our story. The director then points to the invitation God may be extending in this season and helps us explore how we want to respond.

Through a long-term practice of spiritual friendship and spiritual direction, we can learn to put aside the impossible goal of spiritual euphoria without trading it for the dead end of desolation or the loss of genuine faith. Instead, we take on a discipline of honestly telling the story of our lives and experience, with the goal of finding God's presence within the chaos and numbness of life. We receive and weigh the invitations extended to us. We develop the resources to continue forward even when the path is dark—and we learn to feel comfortable navigating the now-familiar path through the dark. More, the journey is no longer alone.

In 2018, my first book was coming out; I had a backlog of emotions, fears, and pent-up spiritual energy tied up in my story. As the release date loomed, I felt an urgent need to get help from someone who was experienced and wise, who could help me discern the leading of the Spirit.

That's when I found Jeff, whom I mentioned earlier. My sessions with him were unhurried and pressure free. He invited me to slow down and to get curious about my own emotions, prayers, and thoughts about God. He helped me navigate the book launch and has continued to accompany me since then, helping me see the movements of both consolation and desolation ebbing and flowing like a symphony in my life. His presence has been an unexpected source of stability and joy.

Have I found the apple-red happiness Catherine sang about growing up? I absolutely have not. But I have learned to not fear the darkness—or despair that it will never end, that God has hidden his face from me and taken my faith away. Instead, I have begun walking those well-worn paths of desolation and consolation with honesty and hope. I've started to know the terrain of these trails, even in the dark.

And I'm convinced now that I never, ever walk alone.

PRACTICE

||||||||||||||||||||||||||||||||||||||||||||||||||||||||||||| *Seeking Spiritual Companionship*

If you were initially sold on a relationship with God because of the supersatisfying emotional side effects, it's likely that you did not learn how to find an honest path forward during low seasons. In the ideas of desolation and consolation there is hope: not that we will find a road around life's valleys of despair but that we will learn to navigate the path that goes through—and learn how to travel with companions.

To begin the practice of spiritual companionship, start with prayer. Ask God to guide you to a spiritual companion who can walk with you on your journey. Maybe it's a friend, or distant mentor. Maybe it's even a family member.

However you answer that question, you may also want to seek out a spiritual director who is a good fit for you. Most Catholic parishes have resources for spiritual direction, but liturgically inclined Protestant churches will too. If there are few good options in your area, many spiritual directors now offer regular direction online.

Whether you find a companion or a spiritual director, you will need to bring honesty and vulnerability to this process. Learn to bring your desolation to God without filter. There is nothing you can say to God that he does not already know, nothing about yourself God does not already hold. But the practice of brutal honesty, desperate seeking, and tentative surrender can be life changing.

Before you begin, take some time to consider what promises for spiritual euphoria you have absorbed. Here are some questions that might lead your reflection:

- What slogans or phrases (i.e., on fire for God) helped form your expectations?
- What are the slogans or phrases that you would use to describe your life with God now?
- What role do you think the fruit of the Spirit plays in your life?
- What negative associations were you taught (or assumed) between depression and disobedience or distance from God? What is your thinking on this now?

To learn more about spiritual direction or to find a spiritual director, here are a few places to start:

- "What Is Spiritual Direction?," a website maintained by MaryKate Morse at Portland Seminary, www.georgefox .edu/seminary/articles/spiritual-direction.html.
- "Find a Spiritual Director," Grafted Life Ministries, www .graftedlife.org/spiritual-direction/find-a-spiritual -director.
- "Find a Spiritual Director," Ignatian Spiritual Exercises, www.ignatianspiritualexercises.com/find-a-spiritual -director/.

|||||||||||||||||||||||||||||||||||||||||||||||||||||||||||||||||||||| *Something to Listen To*

- "Joy," Page CXVI
- "The Rain Keeps Falling," Andrew Peterson
- "Slow Your Breath Down," Future of Forestry

|||||||||||||||||||||||||||||||||||||||||||||||||||||||||||||||||||||| *Something to Read*

- *Sacred Companions: The Gift of Spiritual Friendship Direction*, David G. Benner
- *Spiritual Friendship*, Mindy Caliguire

||||||||||||||||||||||||||||||||||||||||||||||||||||||||||||||||||||||||||||||||||||||||||||||||||||||

PART 3

DEATH
TO LIFE

10

TRADING GREATNESS FOR GOODNESS

My (Catherine's) pager goes off in the middle of the night. I was half expecting it, yet from my REM state I am utterly disoriented. Groping around in the dark I eventually find the small black box, squinting my eyes to read the message, grabbing my phone to dial the number. Sometimes I have to dial three or four times before, in my grogginess, I manage to place the call. I gather a few hurried details from the nurse: This is a "trauma 1" situation. This is going to be rough.

Within five minutes I'm dressed in professional clothes, hair combed and teeth brushed, walking down the snowy street to my car. Twenty minutes later, I swipe my badge to open the door to the emergency department and it begins: my night as a hospital chaplain.[1]

Most of the hospital is dimly lit and sleeping in the wee hours, but the emergency department knows no day or night. These rooms pulse with energy and movement. The patient is a young man who crushed his leg in a horrific construction accident. It's a full room, a dozen people all trained to save lives while staying calm, to complete life-and-death tasks in the midst of chaos. Each person has a job to do, and quickly. Urgently. And what is my job? At the moment, it's to stay present. To hold the man's hand. To help him relax enough to survive—if that's possible.

I lean over him and hold eye contact. "Keep breathing," I say to him again and again. "Take another breath with me." I sound like a midwife or a labor coach. Except, in this case, there is no hope of new life waiting at the end of this long, painful night, only the hope of survival, and so much loss and pain to grapple with in the years to come—if he makes it.

"Focus on my voice!" I say again. "Look at me. I'm here with you." He holds my gaze with an intensity I can never unsee, like an anchor to life. My hand is nearly crushed by the weight of his grip, my heart nearly crushed by the sound of his screams.

Later, as the patient is being transferred to the helicopter that will transport him to a bigger hospital, I walk this man's family out to their car, making sure that in their daze they have understood the directions to their next destination. They're stunned, hardly aware of where they are or what's going on. I've spent an hour with them tonight too, holding the unthinkable thoughts that pour unbidden into their minds.

Finally, it's time for me to head to my own car and begin the sober drive home in the dark. Typically, one call is a lot for one night, yet no sooner do I arrive home than I must turn around and come back. This time, my pager has summoned me to a shocked and grieving family, and I will spend the rest of the night at their side as they receive worse and worse news. Their beloved husband and father had a heart attack at home, then another in the ER, and yet another on the procedure table. As the wee hours tick by, I talk them through the long, long journey from "When can he go home?" to "Is he going to make it?" to "How long should we wait before we take him off life support?"

It is a long night.

It takes me a while, in the morning, to sleep off the exhaustion, to get over the neurons in my brain screaming that being woken in the middle of the night for an emergency is not something that can or should be gotten over by simply driving home to my own house, my own bed. Slowly, I begin to acknowledge that my family is safe, for now. That my life is undisturbed, for now. That I can take a deep breath and quiet my own spirit, for now.

Yet as strange as it sounds, being summoned to these middle-of-the-night traumas feels like blessing to me, one of the most tangible evidences of God's presence and redemption in my life. I cannot bind up wounds or restart hearts, but I know deeply how to show up, to be present with someone in stunning pain, and receive whatever they feel. I know how to sit in the pile of dust and ashes and sit there, and sit there, and sit there.

DEATH AND LIFE

I was asked recently to describe a religious or spiritual symbol that was meaningful to me. I didn't hesitate. I spoke of holding my hands out, cupped together and full of disgusting garbage—or, as we gardeners say, compost. Compost is smelly, gross, and full of bugs. I hate it, and I especially hate it piling up on my kitchen counter, buckets and bowls and pans full of slimy eggshells, apple cores, lettuce hulls, shrimp husks, corn husks.

But eventually, every few days, I convince my husband or sons to carry this smelly, moldy collection out back where it joins an enormous pile, a whole year's worth of garbage. We turn it over, again and again, and eventually something amazing happens: after a long, slow process of decomposing, it becomes rich soil. Suddenly, this death is teeming with life. We spread this black gold on our garden beds by the wheel-barrowful and witness in awe that last year's death has become the womb of new life. The bugs and worms and bacteria did their work; the dense nutrients that remain from those carrot skins and banana peels feed the earth. It's magic.

And then we have a problem, for this womb has burst forth. Thousands and thousands of volunteer plants reach up through the soil, straining for the sun and rain, determined to survive no matter what else we had in mind for that garden bed. I pluck hundreds of tiny volunteer tomato and pepper plants, thousands of tiny lettuce shoots, countless gourds and squash vines, making space for the radishes and onions I've just planted here.

I never, ever, ever tire of watching God, through God's good earth, turn the most rotten death into the most wonderous new life.

Death is stubborn, unrelenting. But so is life. In the most unconducive environment, life fights to survive.

And so do I.

And so do you.

I will keep gardening forever; I will keep letting my husband use all my pans and bowls to collect coffee grounds and moldy apples until no vessels are left for me to cook dinner in, fruit flies and ants crawling and flying all around my house, just so I can watch the long, slow process of life cycling to death and back again to life.

Remember the image of compost in my hands? When I close my eyes, when I lie down on my face before God, this is all I see. I am holding nothing in my hands but all this waste, all this disgusting smelly garbage. And he asks me to open my eyes, to look closer, to see what he sees: a tiny, resilient, oh-so-courageous sprig of green.

All I saw was death. All I brought to him was brokenness. And it has been a long, long time. There have been no shortcuts. No passes. No quick fixes. But I sense the giddy smile on God's face as I peek. God knows how much I love it. The Creator loves it too: new life already beginning.

You could fairly describe me as not quite yet fifty so I have to assume I have reached at least the halfway point of my life. With a significant stretch of road behind me, I can look back now and see that in my suffering God met me, that all my missteps blundering about lost and half blinded by grief led me to here, now, today. Where I am today is not pain free. Neither is it radical success or extreme fulfillment. My days are not Instagram worthy and never picture perfect. I feed my children and sit with the dying. I write words. I do my best to get through each day with what I've been given. I am all too aware that some of the darkest and most terrifying of life's valleys still lie before me. But I am far more deeply rooted than I have ever been before.

Now, with all that road behind me, I have a better sense of what is valuable and worth pursuing, what sparkling things are actually poison and what humble things are deeply alive. I am committed to search for beauty, rest in mystery, chase after love. To admit that the goodness of God is running after me. To provide space and presence for other equally lost and meandering friends, ushering each other to a seat by quiet waters. To take a deep, deep breath of God's presence, of everlasting love, of a goodness that existed long before I was born, that will transcend long after I am gone and forgotten.

I know the value of a spring flower, for I have survived the long, dark hours of winter's death. I know the wonder of a seed placed tenderly in the dirt, for I have walked through valleys of death and know that the only way out is through—and that through leads to new life, if we keep going, if we survive.

I have learned that greatness is a mirage, all too often a smokescreen for something truly empty and toxic—but that goodness and mercy are always following us, if we slow down and let ourselves be overcome. This goodness stems not from leisure and ease but from hard work and persistence, from all that is real and true in life, good and bad, from dirty hands full of garbage and a face lifted to the rising sun.

PSALM 23

In her overnight shifts at the hospital, Catherine often joins a circle of family and friends around their beloved's bedside, keeping vigil together as they watch the patient's heart monitor slowly taper to zero. If they have even a tenuous Christian background, often the family asks her to read from Scripture. More often than not the passage they request is Psalm 23.

When Jason performs memorial services, this psalm is nearly always part of the service. It's hard to imagine facing a funeral or death in which the Lord is not our shepherd, where he isn't present in the darkest valley, leading us through this strange crossing over from life to death. Scripture is rife with pictures of God as a mighty warrior or powerful king, yet this gentle depiction of God is what we choose for the walls of nurseries and hospitals rooms, preschools and funeral homes. In our vulnerable moments we are drawn to this God who describes himself as gentle—a common agricultural nurturer.

The LORD is my shepherd, I lack nothing.
He makes me lie down in green pastures,
he leads me beside quiet waters,
he refreshes my soul.
He guides me along the right paths
for his name's sake. (Psalm 23:1-3)

Coming back to this ancient poem, we realize that the story of this psalm is our story—the whole story. Pull out those worn-out photos one more time: How It Started and How It's Going. What do you see? Whether we come to faith as a child or much later in life, we begin in hope, in faith, in joy. We begin in trust and vulnerability—a lamb taking for granted its life following its shepherd, a trusted protector who provides everything it could need: quiet waters and green pastures, guidance toward the right paths for hope and future.

That's how it started: in the safety of a faith that was first Inherited and then made Confident. We were part of a flock we belonged to. We had what we needed, and it felt like abundant life. We would have stayed there forever.

But then came the darkness.

Even though I walk
    through the darkest valley,
I will fear no evil,
    for you are with me;
your rod and your staff,
    they comfort me. (Psalm 23:4)

This is where we have been traveling together: the darkest valley, or the shadow of death, as some translations say. This is how it's going. Yet even here our ancient brothers and sisters implore us not to give up, or run away. Their voices come to us through generations, encouraging us that God is with us even here, imploring us to continue trusting the shepherd. They ask us to trust so deeply that we find courage to keep walking, even though we are hurting and afraid—because this gentle shepherd is present even in the midst of evil, of suffering.

That rod and staff that bring comfort to the psalmist? Many of us were taught that this shepherding tool was used to beat the errant lamb, to discipline him back into the fold. But in truth, the staff was used to catch the lamb that lost its footing, or recover a lamb that fell behind. The rod was used only to beat away wolves and thieves—including those who misrepresent the gentle faithfulness of God.

This is how the shepherd leads us, fights for us, seeks us, brings us back, keeps us close.

We will at times feel lost, but we are never, ever alone.

How long will we stay here in our mid-faith crisis? There's no way to be sure. We will need time, time to unlearn and learn again. We may need to be comforted. Or we may need space to grieve and heal. There is no one right answer. And there is no rush. The shepherd has all the time in the world. The shepherd can see a faith on the other side of the dark valley and knows how to lead us there.

> You prepare a table before me
>> in the presence of my enemies.
> You anoint my head with oil;
>> my cup overflows.
> Surely your goodness and love will follow me
>> all the days of my life,
> and I will dwell in the house of the LORD forever.
>> (Psalm 23:5-6)

Through these chapters we have looked at ways that our faith—or even ourselves—were unintentionally and unwittingly malformed. Heroes we followed led us astray amid communities that broke rather than healed us. Discipleship inspired us to believe we were somehow exempt from suffering, or elite in our knowledge, or just generally better-than in God's eyes. One thing that links all these catalysts of crisis is the false promises, false teachers, and false paths that implicitly guaranteed us greatness. Armed with truth and power, we would do great things for God! God would do great things for us! The full brunt of life's suffering would not touch us for we were in God's hands!

But the real promise of faith is not greatness but goodness. Jesus did not invite his followers to take up their crowns and go to the palace. Rather, he implored them to take up their crosses and kneel on the ground to wash dirty feet, becoming people known for love and service even in the face of persecution and death. Because God is this way. In Jesus, the people who were not allowed to form an image of God to aid their worship saw the true image of God: Jesus, washing our feet. Jesus, dying for his enemies. Jesus, being laid in the ground in surrender to death yet rising again in new life to bring healing to the very ones who killed him.

If we are to continue forward, one thing we must do is lay aside those noisy, chaotic, false hopes for greatness and turn instead to seek God's goodness on a path of peace and humility. We must be willing to sit and eat at a table with our enemies.

At this table the shepherd has set, there is no fear, no shame, and no VIP section. Rather, there is goodness, mercy, loving-kindness. Here we find the peace of resting in mystery; the delight of coming home; the occasional glimpses of God's presence, never fully, never clearly but through a glass dimly. Enough to follow us all the days of our complicated, beautiful, terrifying, precious lives.

In the house of the Lord, we will know our own frailty and feel the fact of our mortality. We will see enemies around us: the heartbreaks still ahead, the lingering doubts and dead ends, the injustices that feel intractable. And yet, God invites us to

Conscious Faith, where we sit and rest and receive at the table, in the presence of all this.

I (Jason) have a friend who has found this table, who has learned how to sit in God's presence and goodness, even in the midst of tragedy. Ron spent decades teaching kids and mentoring teenagers in his community. He has no platform. He has no podcast, no books to his name, and no pulpit (despite people's best efforts to make him a pastor), but everybody in town has a Ron story. When I meet other pastors from his town, they tell me about a time when crisis and tragedy struck, and Ron was there, offering comfort and helping the survivors forge a way forward. Others talk of their own troubles and how Ron sat across from them, tears in his eyes, and whispered grace.

That grace doesn't flow from an easy life. This man has dealt with a relentless barrage of health problems. In the last few years alone, he's undergone knee and hip replacements, not to mention a host of severe health problems from his heart to his kidneys. But the gravitas he carries stems back further, to a different kind of pain.

Decades ago, when he was twenty-seven years old, Ron stood in front of his sixth-grade classroom, beaming, as his students gave their best guesses on the size and weight of his new baby, due to arrive that very night. But the child was born with massive health complications. The doctor could not save him. Ron and his wife got to hold their son for little more than an hour before saying goodbye. The next day, Ron was back with his students, weeping with them in front of the chalkboard predictions.

Ron's commitment to authenticity and gentleness was present even then in the midst of crisis, but it has grown more pronounced over the years. Contrary to the false promises of greatness, youth, and fame, people are more drawn to Ron now in his obscurity and mature age. Not because he knows all the answers, but because he knows how to hold the painful questions with great care. Grace and goodness flow freely over him. His cup runneth over. Ron has lifted up to God the compost of his life—all that is broken and lost—and found new life growing in the midst of it.

There are so many others we've met who are like Ron, so many who survived years or decades of trouble and crisis and now sit at the table of Conscious Faith. Their suffering has not ended, and yet they have found something more, something true, something real. And they are more than ready to show us the way, if we can slow down long enough to take a seat beside them.

When Catherine is called to attend patients awaiting death, she hears a similar refrain echoed again and again: Did I love well? Was I a good spouse, a good parent, a good friend?

The urgency she sees in their faces and feels in the squeeze of their hands on hers belies what really matters to us in the end. However much greatness we may achieve, it is goodness we reach for at the last: Did I love well? Have I given them all the love they need to continue on without me? Am I surrounded by their love for my final breaths?

It is not our great works that will plant these seeds in the years and decades before harvest, friend. It is the hardships we endure together, the experience of walking all the way through deep, dark valleys and coming out the other side and finding we are not alone, have never, ever been alone. It is in giving and receiving faithful, steadfast love and mercy.

This is where we hope to end up: surrounded by love and goodness, all the days of our lives. But for now, all that is required of us is to not give up. To keep on going even in the darkest valley. How? By looking forward in trust that the Lord is our shepherd. After life and faith have knocked us down so many times, we aren't still following God to achieve greatness or safety but to find beauty and meaning in the quiet, humble pasture, in the wisdom of maturity, in the mixed-bag blessing of community, in the indescribable wonder of love.

The Lord is our shepherd. And so we walk with him.

It is a long journey, friend. Faith is the trip, and the task, of a lifetime. We will become tired and discouraged. We will want to give up at times. Sometimes we will give up and need a hand or two to carry us for a while. Occasionally, we will need to sit down in the dust and ashes for a long, long time. But remember, real growth comes through winter and spring, dormancy and life, seasons of suffering and seasons of peace. New life comes from the garbage and death we have offered up to God and the long, slow process of time.

Even on those hard days, we do not walk alone. Rather, we walk together, and hope is free for the lending. We share our stories; we share reasons to stay on the path. And the goodness of the shepherd calls to us, urges us to keep moving, keep going, keep putting one foot in front of the other.

Let's keep walking together, friend. Even when our strength runs out, perhaps our hope will not. And surely, we will dwell in the house of the Lord forever.

PRACTICE

Trading Greatness for Goodness

As you consider trading a pursuit of greatness for a path of goodness, here a few questions to consider:

- Earlier in your life, where did you expect to find meaning and fulfillment?
- Now that you're a bit further in, where do you find meaning and fulfillment?
- Take a moment in silence to look back on your life so far. Bring up memories that feel like treasures as well as those that feel like garbage. Offer up each one. If it helps, consider journaling or drawing some of the things that come to mind. From your current place on the path, what do you see now that you couldn't see at the time?
- Think about who you know that fits the description of someone who has found the rootedness that comes after the crisis. What do you notice in this person? What stands out? What would you like to aim for in this picture?

Something to Listen To

- "Goodness of God," Jenn Johnson
- "Farther Along," Josh Garrels
- "The House of God Forever," Jon Foreman

EPILOGUE

Catherine and I inadvertently picked a terrible year to write this book. While she was working through seminary, starting chaplaincy, and dealing with a barrage of personal and family crises, I was training to be a spiritual director and dealing with my own barrage of crises. The amount of fresh drama we walked through felt almost comical at times. "Really??" we'd say when we touched base and exchanged updates. "Another hard thing?" But it wasn't actually funny. Those mounting troubles only exacerbated my own ongoing mid-faith crisis.

People like to use the word *deconstruction* for seasons like these, but it feels more like demolition as our spiritual lives get stripped down to the studs. Questions come like sledgehammers, taking out old modes of belief, removing cracked assumptions and broken platitudes that can no longer bear the weight of reality. Then we must tear out all the old idols—people we thought were pillars of the faith, answers we thought could stand the test of pain. We're left with no heroes to worship and no illusions to indulge in. The only solid thing we have left is the expectation of more pain.

That was me. I was still holding onto Jesus, still writing this book. By now, I knew he would walk with me into the next stage of faith, but it was hard to imagine how that stage could contain anything but sorrow. I was willing to keep following the Shepherd, but I was struggling.

Then, in the middle of our writing, something unexpected happened: a plot twist that forever changed the way I see our spiritual journey. Though it was personal to my life, this development was so significant that I owe it to you, dear reader, to share it here before we say goodbye.

I've already told you how much I longed to know the inner world of my autistic son Jack. This has been the greatest desire of my adult life. I wanted to see a miracle; I wanted to hear his voice. But I laid down that desire.

A week after I made that decision, I preached a sermon and told the story of my afternoon with Jack at Buffalo Wild Wings. "There were no words between us," I recounted. "But I was okay with that, you know? Most of my life with him I wasn't okay with that, but I was now. Because I finally realized I had something better than words: presence." It was a stake-in-the-ground moment of acceptance. Jack would never talk, but that was okay. I loved my son and finally understood we didn't need words to know one another.

That same afternoon, I awoke from my post-sermon nap to a text pointing me to a documentary about a new, ultra-low-tech therapy that promised to unlock language for people like Jack. I rolled my eyes at first. People always send me stuff like this. But this time it was my mom, so I clicked on the link and watched the documentary.[1] The explanation was so simple, so promising, and made so much sense that I felt scared. Hope, as I've written before, is a terrifying thing for me. My wife and I watched with tears pouring down our cheeks.

Two weeks later, Jack and I sat in a small Portland office where a calm and confident woman looked into my son's eyes and said, "I know you're smart." We understood that she was defying the doctors who had deemed him intellectually disabled. "I know you're in there. I know you've been watching and listening to everything around you for seventeen years. But your body is working against you. And we're going to help you communicate."

I wanted to believe it. But we had been through too many rounds of false hope. Too many diets, too many therapies, too many short bursts of communication that fizzled in a week or two. Still, the more she talked, the more sense she made of everything we had experienced with Jack.

We went all in.

Over the next few months, Jack proved the woman right. Yes, he had nonverbal autism, but he was not cognitively impaired. Not at all. Rather, he had a condition called apraxia. Like a stroke victim, his mind was intact, but his body was a wild card. He lacked the basic motor control that allows the rest of us to communicate basic needs, let alone demonstrate our intelligence. So we began actively training his motor skills.

Within two months, we started to see things, amazing things. By rigorously practicing simple movements in his arm and shoulder every day, Jack gained enough motor control to point accurately to large letters on a plastic alphabet stencil. The practitioner would ask him simple questions based on paragraphs she had just read out loud, and he would slowly, slowly spell out simple answers, pointing to one letter at a time. After two months, she started asking questions to test his prior knowledge, information he had picked up outside of these sessions. I will never forget the one that made me a believer.

"Jack, do you know who coined the term 'Iron Curtain'?"

I personally had no idea who coined the term, but Jack didn't hesitate. He took the pencil and pointed to the big letters one by one, spelling out the name, "W-I-N-S-T-O-N C-H-U-R-C-H-I-L-L."

I sat up straight and shot her a questioning look.

She grinned at me. Her eyes said, "I told you."

This was just the beginning. In the subsequent weeks, Jack demonstrated a broad knowledge of history and geography, math and science, sports and religion. He calculated the area of Stonehenge, listed the US presidents in order, and quoted easily from the Psalms, the book of Acts, and the Gospel of John.

After each session, I would text the transcripts to Catherine. Her responses always came back in all caps. "JASON. WHAT. IS. HAPPENING."

What was happening was Jack finally getting a chance to prove his intelligence and prodigious memory—to allow just a tiny sliver of what was in his head to escape and reach us on the outside.

"Jack, in your own words, tell me what a patent is."

He took his pencil and spelled out this gem: "A patent is a form of protection manufacturers use to keep their products safe from competitors."

"Jack, what is the poet Virgil's masterpiece called?"

"The Aeneid."

"Jack, what did Ronald Reagan say to Gorbachev in Berlin?"

"Tear down this wall."

Indeed. "Tear down this wall." How's that for poetry?

My other children were as aghast as we were by all this. "Dad, I think Jack is smarter than me," his brother Sam said one day.

"Bud, I think he's smarter than me too."

Two months later, when Jack's accuracy and confidence had risen, he reached what we call "open communication"—using his own words to make sentences that made paragraphs to tell us anything that was on his mind, rather than merely answering prompts about factual data. For the first time in his life, he described to us what was going on inside him: How his body does things out of his control. How the stimuli around him assault his senses. How he has felt trapped inside his own body for the past seventeen years. How sweet it was to be able to finally speak, even in this modified form.

"I am so thankful for you," he spelled out to his practitioner, after six months of hard work. "You saved my life."

Eventually, he requested that we pull him out of the private school he was attending so he could take high school classes online.[2]

This story continues to unfold. Every week, I learn more about my son, about his history of pain, and his desires for the future. He recently started his own blog to advocate for other nonspeakers, to help them find their voice the way he found his. And he wants to go to college someday to study astrophysics.

Don't get me wrong: this isn't a Hollywood ending. We don't have everything we dreamed; Jack still very much wishes he could speak and interact in a typical way. He may never have that. But at the same time, I could never have predicted Jack's dramatic turn from sadness into joy. I never imagined his silent life would suddenly overflow with language. Indeed, I've struggled to find words of my own to talk about it. But the very fact that it took me by surprise has become a fresh source of hope for me in thinking about my own mid-faith crisis.

Recently, a woman in my church named Shannon shared about how, in the midst of hardships, curiosity became a source of joy. She said that in stressful seasons, her mindset gets closed and fatalistic. She finds herself rehearsing all the ways her sorrows will probably multiply and nothing will end well. Soon, every concern becomes a dead end, and joy itself sounds like one of those flimsy fantasies someone promised us from a pulpit once upon a time.

Curiosity, however, does the opposite: it makes her world larger. When she embraces curiosity, she starts seeing God as a big God, who is not only good but also creative and infinitely resourceful. Time and again, she says, God has turned sorrow into joy, heartbreak into glory, but the path to those blessings is never predictable.

This concept rings true for me. When my mid-faith crisis first hit, I had to give up the false promises of security and greatness. I felt empty, as if all that was left was fatalism: the promise of pain, with the consolation prize that at least Christ would share in it with me. In this life, I would have troubles. I know. I know. I know.

But then came the twist. I was, to steal a phrase from C. S. Lewis, surprised by joy. I discovered there was more than sorrow on this journey. There was more than pain.

I never saw it coming.

What if we embraced this gift of curiosity in the midst of our crisis? What if we became like children again, not demanding specific outcomes but believing that this big God we follow might yet amaze us somehow? After all, if Christ can turn water to wine, surely he can turn some of our ashes into beauty. Surely he can surprise us once in a while.

Curiosity is not, and will never be, an antidote to pain. But I have found it to be a balm. For while we walk through hardship, the God of the unexpected walks with us. That means there will be beautiful surprises right next to the hard ones. I've seen it with my own eyes, in my beloved son.

Jack sat down with us one morning, and we held up the letterboard and asked him how he felt. He told us, "I am filled with hope."

The Very Big Things I spent years asking God for did not materialize in the ways I asked for or expected. But surely, God heard my cry and answered me. No, greatness hasn't found me, and I no longer expect or even hope that it will, because, surely, God's goodness has.

ACKNOWLEDGMENTS

Thank you, Don Gates, for your advocacy and excitement. Thank you, Al Hsu and the team at InterVarsity Press, for helping us shape this book and bring it to life. We are deeply grateful to Gene and Linda Carlson (Catherine's parents), to John and Sophia, and to the many other friends who let us share their stories. Thanks to the pastoral staff of Christ's Center Church for giving Jason the flexibility to work on this book (and to the good folks at Zoom for allowing us to restart our meetings every forty minutes). Thanks to Jeff Savage for meeting Jason at ground zero in his crisis of faith. Thanks to Matthew (Catherine's husband) for helping us start on the right foot, and to Sara (Jason's wife) for listening to his incessant verbal processing over the thornier chapters.

Thank you to our friends and spiritual companions who have met us for coffee and taken our phone calls in the best and worst years of our lives. You know who you are. We are grateful for the great cloud of witnesses who wrestled questions and doubts and passed on the wisdom they won in the process.

Finally, thank you to our Good Shepherd: You have the words of eternal life.

NOTES

1. LET'S START WITH A MEME

[1]Ernie Rettino, composer, "Stand Up," featuring Debby Kerner Rettino and Psalty, Rettino/Kerner Pub., 1982, psalty.com/track/687860/stand-up.

2. STAGES OF FAITH

[1]James W. Fowler, *Stages of Faith: The Psychology of Human Development and the Quest for Meaning* (San Francisco: Harper & Row, 1981); Janet O. Hagberg and Robert A. Guelich, *The Critical Journey: Stages in the Life of Faith*, 2nd ed. (Salem, WI: Sheffield, 2005); M. Scott Peck, *The Road Less Traveled: A New Psychology of Love, Traditional Values and Spiritual Growth* (New York: Simon & Schuster, 1978); and Brian D. McLaren, *Finding Faith: A Self-discovery Guide for Your Spiritual Quest* (Grand Rapids, MI: Zondervan, 1999).

[2]Walter Brueggemann, *Praying the Psalms: Engaging Scripture and the Life of the Spirit*, 2nd ed. (Eugene, OR: Cascade Books, 2007), 2.

[3]It's important to note that this beginning and the trajectory are true across a wide spectrum of religious and even nonreligious backgrounds and are not limited to the Christian faith.

3. WHEN DOUBT CREPT IN

[1]*Peter Pan*, directed by P. J. Hogan, Universal Pictures, 2003.

[2]Teresa, *Mother Teresa: Come Be My Light; The Private Writings of the "Saint of Calcutta,"* ed. Brian Kolodiejchuk (New York: Doubleday, 2007), 187.

[3]Catherine McNiel, *All Shall Be Well: Awakening to God's Presence in His Messy, Abundant World* (Colorado Springs, CO: NavPress, 2019).

[4]C. S. Lewis, *The Silver Chair*, Complete Chronicles of Narnia (New York: Harper-Collins, 1998), 432.

[5]Anne Lamott, *Plan B: Further Thoughts on Faith* (New York: Penguin Random House, 2006), 256-57.

4. WHEN CHURCH WAS HARMFUL

[1]Jenn Johnson, "Goodness of God," by Jenn Johnson, Ed Cash, Jason Ingram, Ben Fielding, and Brian Johnson, *Victory*, Bethel Music, 2019.

5. WHEN OUR HEROES FELL

[1]Ray Sanchez, "Famed Evangelist Ravi Zacharias Engaged in Sexual Misconduct, His Ministry Says," *Crime + Justice*, CNN, February 12, 2021, www.cnn.com/2021/02/12/us/ravi-zacharias-sexual-misconduct-report/index.html; and Daniel Silliman, "Ravi Zacharias's Ministry Investigates Claims of Sexual Misconduct at Spas," *Christianity Today*, September 29, 2020, www.christianitytoday.com/news/2020/september/ravi-zacharias-sexual-harassment-rzim-spa-massage-investiga.html.

[2]Megan Cornwell, "Ravi Zacharias' Sins of Sexual Abuse Went Undetected for Years," *Premier Christianity*, January 27, 2023, www.premierchristianity.com/features/ravi-zacharias-sins-of-sexual-abuse-went-undetected-for-years-here-are-the-lessons-the-church-needs-to-learn/14737.article.

[3]Reuters, "Hillsong Founder Resigns After Church Finds Evidence of Misconduct," *NBC News*, March 23, 2022, www.nbcnews.com/news/world/hillsong-church-brian-houston-resigns-rcna21133; Craig Welch, "The Rise and Fall of Mars Hill Church," Local News, *Seattle Times*, pub. September 13, 2014, updated February 4, 2016, www.seattletimes.com/seattle-news/the-rise-and-fall-of-mars-hill-church/; Louisa Marshall, "What Was Bill Gothard Accused Of?: Inside Sexual Abuse Claims Against Duggar IBLP Religious Leader," *InTouch*, Y!Entertainment, May 18, 2023, www.yahoo.com/entertainment/bill-gothard-accused-inside-sexual-194402162.html; and "A Chronicle Investigation: Abuse of Faith," *Houston Chronicle*, 2019, www.houstonchronicle.com/news/investigations/abuse-of-faith/.

[4]Mariah Espada, "*The Secrets of Hillsong* Explores How the Megachurch Attracted Celebrities," *Time*, May 19, 2023, https://time.com/6281346/hillsong-documentary-celebrities-fx/.

6. WHEN OUR PRAYERS FELL SILENT

[1]See Luke 5:17-26.

[2]Brian Johnson, Joel Case, and Jonathan David Hessler, "No Longer Slaves," Bethel Music, 2014.

[3]Teresa, *Teresa of Avila: The Book of Her Life*, trans. Kieran Kavanaugh and Otilio Rodriguez in *Collected Works of St. Teresa of Avila* (Washington, DC: Institute of Carmelite Studies, 1976), 1:67.

[4]"The Ignatian Examen," Jesuit Conference of Canada and the U.S., www.jesuits .org/spirituality/the-ignatian-examen/.

[5]"Jesus Prayer—Prayer of the Heart," Prayer of the Orthodox Church, Archdiocese of N.A., Saint George Cathedral, www.orthodoxprayer.org/Jesus%20 Prayer.html.

7. WHEN SUFFERING CONSUMED US

[1]"Ears to Hear," *The Chosen*, created by Dallas Jenkins, season 3, episode 7, Loaves & Fishes Productions, 2023.

[2]Malcolm Guite, "Lent with Herbert Day 7: Engine Against th'Almightie," March 5, 2020, https://malcolmguite.wordpress.com/2020/03/05/lent-with -herbert-day-7-engine-against-thalmightie/. Used by permission.

[3]Maria Shriver, "Maria Shriver Interviews the Famously Private Poet Mary Oliver," *OWN*, Oprah.com, March 9, 2011, www.oprah.com/entertainment /maria-shriver-interviews-poet-mary-oliver/all.

[4]Liza Wieland, "Why Do We Ignore the Suffering in the Poems of Mary Oliver and Elizabeth Bishop?," *Literary Hub*, June 28, 2019, https://lithub.com /why-do-we-ignore-the-suffering-in-the-poems-of-mary-oliver-and-elizabeth -bishop/.

[5]Krista Tippett, "Mary Oliver: 'I Got Saved by the Beauty of the World,'" *On Being*, aired February 5, 2015, updated March 31, 2022, https://onbeing.org /programs/mary-oliver-i-got-saved-by-the-beauty-of-the-world/.

[6]Shriver, "Maria Shriver Interviews the Famously Private Poet Mary Oliver."

[7]Gregory A. Boyd and Edward K. Boyd, *Letters from a Skeptic: A Son Wrestles with His Father's Questions About Christianity* (Colorado Springs, CO: Cook, 2008), 76-77.

8. WHEN OUR BELIEFS COLLAPSED

[1]A.C.E. School of Tomorrow, www.aceschooloftomorrow.com.

[2]Saji George, "Tom's Doubts #14," https://twitter.com/S_A_J_I/status/11004008 7445782528.

9. WHEN FEELINGS FADED

[1]Warren Watkins, "Apple-Red Happiness," Lillenas, 1977.

[2]George William Cooke, "Joy in My Heart," 1884.

[3]*The Office*, created by Greg Daniels, season 6, episode 12, "Scott's Tots," Deedle-Dee Productions, original air date December 3, 2009, NBC, www.peacocktv.com/watch/playback/vod/GMO_00000000001659_01/38eb7a3c-dfab-378a-bad5-493e82d3a64d.

[4]Ignatius of Loyola, *The Spiritual Exercises of Saint Ignatius*, ed. Brian McDermott (Dreamscape Media, 2018), 143, Kindle.

[5]Ignatius of Loyola, *Spiritual Exercises*, 144.

[6]Teresa, *Mother Teresa: Come Be My Light; The Private Writings of the "Saint of Calcutta,"* ed. Brian Kolodiejchuk (New York: Doubleday, 2007), 169, 63.

[7]*Mother Teresa: Come Be My Light*, 158, 149.

[8]Billy Gaines and Sarah Gaines, "You Are Faithful, Lord," by Billy Gaines and John G. Elliott, *Billy & Sarah Gaines*, track 2, Benson Records, 1986.

[9]"Spiritual Direction," *IgnatianSpirituality.com*, Loyal Press, accessed September 14, 2024, www.ignatianspirituality.com/making-good-decisions/spiritual-direction/.

10. TRADING GREATNESS FOR GOODNESS

[1]Details of these incidents have been changed for the sake of privacy.

EPILOGUE

[1]*SPELLERS: The Movie*, Spellers Freedom Foundation, 2023, www.spellersfreedomfoundation.org/spellers-the-movie, www.youtube.com/watch?v=8h1rcLyznK0.

[2]Jason Hague, "My Non-Speaking, Autistic Teenage Son Has a Communication Breakthrough," Dec. 16, 2023, www.youtube.com/watch?v=A_-zc-3p_ew.

ABOUT THE AUTHORS

Catherine and Jason forged a friendship over LEGO Batman quotes, texting about Toblerone chocolate, and arguing about Ted Lasso. Before ever meeting in person, they cowrote and published a postapocalyptic short story. Now, they write books together about despair, disillusionment, and spiritual dead ends.

Connect with them at:
https://catherinemcniel.com/
https://www.jasonhague.com/

Like this book?

Scan the code to discover more content like this!

Get on IVP's email list to receive special offers, exclusive book news, and thoughtful content from your favorite authors on topics you care about.

ivp | InterVarsity Press